HOW TO

GET MORE

LAW FIRM

CLIENTS

Without Losing Time & Money or Getting
SCREWED By a Marketing Company

ANDREW STICKEL

How to Get More Law Firm Clients Without Losing Time & Money or Getting Screwed By a Marketing Company Copyright © 2019 by Andrew Stickel

ISBN: 9781790417957
Imprint: Independently published

Printed in the United States of America

This publication is designed to provide accurate and authoritative information with regard to the subject matter covered. It is sold with the understanding that neither the author nor publisher is engaged in rendering legal, accounting, or other professional advice. If legal advice or other expert assistance is required, the services of a competent professional person should be sought.

Before we go any further, I want you to see that I'm not your average internet marketer—I know my stuff. Let me introduce you to several real lawyers who've achieved real, tangible results from my law firm marketing and advertising strategies.

 Joseph Simon 💬 recommends Andrew Stickel.
13 hrs · 🌐

Andy Stickel is an amazing marketer! Listen to this man, he knows what he is talking about!

 Carlo Cocuzzi 💬 recommends Andrew Stickel.
January 4 · 🌐

Andrew absolutely knows how to get leads for lawyers. His strategies are helping me grow two lawyer firms in the UK. Thank you!!

 Jason Guy Andy Stickel is the man! I sat by him at a mastermind once. He was attending just like I was but in one of his comments we all just started staring at him and taking turns asking questions about how to generate leads. 6 weeks later I saw him get an award from Russell Bronson for outperforming 97% of the other advertisers in that room (about 5000). Throw your money at Andy and watch your business grow!

Like · Reply · Message · 15h   👍 1

 Josh Nelson 💬 recommends Andrew Stickel.
2 mins · 🌐

As a small law firm owner time is definitely one of my scarcest resources but working with Andy's content has been an effective way for me to use some of my downtime in the car to listen to his videos and take actionable steps to get more potential clients in for consults which results in me being able to help more families protect themselves and the ones they love

 James Kim 💬 recommends Andrew Stickel.
August 29 at 5:38 PM · 🌐

Andrew Stickel's strategies increased profit and ROI for our business. Highly recommend him to anyone looking to improve profitability!

 Denise Adkison-Brown reviewed Andrew Stickel —   💬 ···

July 23, 2018 · 🌐

His advice and recommendations are always great, thorough, and easy to follow. I've been implementing his ideas and I am starting to see results.

Mandy Moyer 💬 recommends Andrew Stickel.
October 10, 2018 · 🌐

Andy is passionate about helping entrepreneurs (including lawyers like me!) market their services in innovative ways, and his tips are EXCELLENT! Most importantly, he communicates those tips in an easily digestible format (videos, which can be played while multitasking). Any time I stop by for new insight, I leave with at least one piece of actionable content. Seriously, Andy's great!! #teamandy

 Jefre Goldtrap 💬 recommends Andrew Stickel.
November 12, 2018 · 🌐

Andrew provides quality products. That being said he is not all sell, sell, sell. He offers volumes of helpful content and takes the time to answer questions. A+ work. Highly recommend him.

 Brad Woolley reviewed Andrew Stickel — 5★
Just now · 🌐

Andy is always posting very informative marketing strategies to help lawyers like myself get leads. His videos are very easy to understand and follow. If you implement his ideas, you should see an increase in clients.

 Paul Vincent 💬 recommends Andrew Stickel.
August 16 · 🌐

Andrew is a hustler and knows his stuff. If you're interested in marketing by a different means than the traditional old fashioned way, then reach out to Andrew and his company.

 Josh Nelson 💬 recommends Andrew Stickel.
2 mins · 🌐

As a small law firm owner time is definitely one of my scarcest resources but working with Andy's content has been an effective way for me to use some of my downtime in the car to listen to his videos and take actionable steps to get more potential clients in for consults which results in me being able to help more families protect themselves and the ones they love

 Allison Williams 💬 recommends Andrew Stickel.
July 23 · 🌐

Andy Stickel gives great content for lawyers seeking to grow their law firms through strategic marketing initiatives. He's full of information, entertaining, accessible and a great resource for lawyers. As a business coach for lawyers, I highly recommend his services. #NeverStopGrowing

Larry Garfinkel 📣 recommends Andrew Stickel.
July 23 · 🌐

Andrew is a wealth of great marketing information. I was unclear how his system could work in my practice area so I sent him an email and the next day he posted a video that answered my question in detail. I tried what he suggested and it is working. I highly recommend him and his Facebook group as well.

 Chip Cossé 🖐 I would definitely recommend all lawyers attend this training. Andy is always spot on with his marketing strategies and light years ahead of the competition. I have tried, failed and wasted untold sums with other companies. They rely on ppc as a security blanket. Andy has unlocked the Holy Grail of organic lead generation, resulting in higher client conversion at a greatly reduced acquisition cost. He's a genius in his field and has the rare ability to translate unique or otherwise complex subjects into easily understood methods and he and his staff are always available to guide you, if needed.

Like · Reply · 2h   👍 1

 Russ Nesevich I learn more from him in a 10-minute phone call than I could in weeks of research. he's a wealth of knowledge. don't miss out on this.

 Mariana Burgos I attempted Facebook Ads for our firm. I might as well have thrown money out of the car on the freeway. It wasn't until I saw Andy Stickel's YouTube videos until I realized what I was doing wrong!
Worth every second. I highly suggest watching it a few times as he has so much knowledge.

Like · Reply · 5w   👍 1

 Evan Sauer 🖐 Increased my leads by 500% after doing one FB Live for an influencer's group. Thanks Andy Stickel your strategies work and are changing my business!

Like · Reply · 37m   👍 1

 Michael Samuel Evan Sauer Andy Stickel knows his stuff!

Like · Reply · 1m

Patrick J. McGeehan 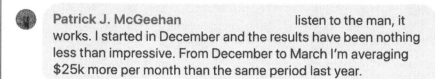 listen to the man, it works. I started in December and the results have been nothing less than impressive. From December to March I'm averaging $25k more per month than the same period last year.

Like · Reply · 2w

Andy Stickel ⬢ Patrick J. McGeehan that's amazing, Patrick! Which strategies have you found to work the best?

Like · Reply · 2d

Patrick J. McGeehan Andy Stickel I fired my marketing agency, got myself listed on page one of google (with a Regis office), post daily on social media, post 2-3 videos a week, and constantly update my page. In the beginning it took a few hours to get it up and running but now my system takes about 15 minutes a day.

Glenn Mcgovern Andy--I have more good motorcycle death cases in less than two months of effort with just one idea of yours. I am still working on the whole strategy implementation.

Like · Reply · 16h

 Andy Stickel Glenn Mcgovern How many cases did you get? That's Great to hear

Like · Reply · 15h

Glenn Mcgovern I got 4 new cases and out of the 4 two are death cases.

Like · Reply · 15h   👍 1

What's Next?

www.getlawfirmclients.com/training

Go beyond the book! This free training reveals how any lawyer can get more clients using one simple advertising strategy.

Just show up on the web class, and you'll receive a fully functioning law firm landing page template ($5,000 value) for free! Just plug in your info and go.

www.getlawfirmclients.com/training

Get a free MP3 player with audio from over one hundred of my YouTube marketing videos. Headphones Included!

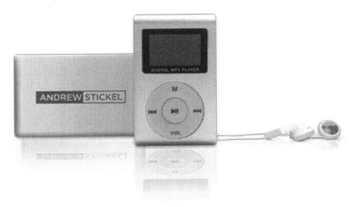

All you have to do is record a video testimonial telling me how this book helps you. Then go to mp3.andrewstickel.com, upload your video, and fill out the form.

A lot of times people want to leave a review but aren't quite sure what to say. Below are some questions that should give you some ideas and will make your review more helpful to other lawyers reading the book.

1. What was the problem you had before you read this book?

2. Why did you choose this book?

3. What makes this book so effective?

4. As a result of implementing the strategies in this book, what was your outcome?

5. How has your life changed since achieving this outcome?

The more detail you can provide the better, but if you're short on time or inspiration I'd still love a shorter review.

Contents

Chapter 1
The Secret to Getting More Law Clients

Renee's Story

"How many lawyers do you know who start a law firm while sleeping on a friend's couch?" Renee asked me.

"You're the first," I said. "Tough job prospects right now?"

"Some lawyers find a job right after graduating law school. That's not my story." Renee shook her head. "But I didn't give up. I *knew* I could do it."

When Renee started out, she didn't have a website. She didn't have an advertising budget. She had nothing except her time, her laptop, and a new marketing idea—one very few lawyers knew about.

"Most lawyers try to grow their law firms by talking about themselves," I said. "You've seen their TV ads and billboards. They talk about their years of experience, cases won, or settlement amounts."

"Which I don't have yet."

"...or *need*, apparently." I smiled.

"Apparently."

"People are pretty simple," I said. "We're always going around thinking, '*What's in it for me?*' We ask that about everything."

"Including law firm ads," Renee said. "Only problem is, most lawyers never answer that question. They *assume* people already know what lawyers like me can do for them. So, all I do is answer questions and educate people. Not only have people started trusting me, but a few even asked about my services!"

"Even though you're just starting out?"

"Even though I'm just starting out." She repeated. "I've only been at this for a few months. Other lawyers have been in the business thirty or forty years!"

"So, how do you do it?"

"Well, my dream clients have always been online entrepreneurs," Renee said. "I knew they needed help with legal issues around starting and running a business."

"Other lawyers are probably targeting that market with the typical 'hire me, hire me' ads all the time. How did you swoop in, differentiate yourself, and provide value?"

"Like I said, it started with answering their legal questions," she said. "Did you know there are countless social media groups that consist solely of online entrepreneurs? They were perfect for me."

Renee gave me the whole scoop. She joined a dozen of these social media groups and read the members' comments—*and* questions.

"Do you guys have your freelancers sign contracts?"

"What needs to be in my ecommerce business' operating agreement?"

"I'm worried about people stealing my Intellectual Property. Do I need to register a trademark?"

Just like that, Renee had found them—her dream clients needing legal guidance. But she didn't blast the groups with posts offering her services on retainer. Instead, she hopped in on the conversations, answering questions and offering advice for free.

People *loved* it. And they wanted more. As Renee's answers got longer and more detailed, she started turning them into articles and posting them directly into other groups. One of her first posts was a legal checklist for online entrepreneurs. This resource made it easy to understand what legal steps to take when starting an ecommerce business.

Renee came up with more ideas by reading entrepreneurs' questions. If she spotted a common misconception about a certain topic (like trademark law), she wrote an article. If more than one person posted the same question, she tackled it in the next one. Within a few weeks, *thousands* of entrepreneurs viewed Renee as their go-to person for legal help. And then they turned into *paying clients*. Several group administrators even asked her to take a more active role by hosting live video Q&A sessions—which got her even more clients.

After six months of this new marketing strategy, Renee called me with an update.

"You're not going to believe it!" she said. "I've signed *twenty* retainer clients doing this. All I've had to do is answer questions and provide value. I started out spending a few hours everyday finding these groups, writing content, and interacting with members. But now? People see me as an authority on legal matters, so I only have to spend about ten minutes per day on this strategy."

"That's awesome!" I said. "But I'm not surprised. When you show up and provide value *first*, you build a bond with people that traditional advertising can't buy."

"Get this—" she said. "I still haven't spent a dime on marketing, and I now have a *six figure* law firm."

"Six figures in six months."

"...and my own place." Renee smiled. *"Finally!"*

It's a common misconception that marketing a law firm is expensive and time-consuming. As Renee's story proves, lawyers don't need massive marketing budgets (or huge marketing agencies) to achieve results. With a little hard work—and a few innovative marketing ideas—lawyers can grow their practice in no time. Except most don't. After many years of helping lawyers use the internet to get more law clients, I've learned a dirty little secret:

Every lawyer wants results like Renee, but the marketing strategies they follow won't *ever* get them there.

Here's why.

Law Firm Marketing Mistakes (You're Probably Making)

Marketing is always evolving. Forty years ago, lawyers couldn't advertise. Then along came Bates v. Arizona State Bar, and attorneys rushed to radio stations, local TV, and the phone book to find that once-in-a-lifetime case. Then the internet happened, bringing us Search Engine Optimization (SEO), Pay Per Click (PPC) ads, and most recently, social media.

Every lawyer I talk to has tried one (or more) of these, but most felt like they were just throwing money away. And they were. Here's what they didn't understand—most advertising platforms are what marketing professors W. Chan Kim and Renée Mauborgne call "Red Oceans." Like bloody waters full of sharks all feeding on the same fish, these platforms are ultra-competitive.

Take SEO, for example. How many other lawyers in your market are now competing for that top spot on Google? Or that top PPC spot, where you're having to pay $100 to $200 a click?

Many lawyers invest in one expensive ad campaign, hoping a single ad will be a home run. Sometimes that works. Sometimes a blind squirrel finds a nut. But not often. Even if your one-off ad *does* book appointments on your calendar, you then have to invest in follow up advertising called remarketing.

Imagine a person comes into your law firm for a consultation. You have a nice conversation, they sound interested, but then they disappear and never return your call. What happened to them? Well, most people get caught up in life. Work, kids, you name it. Even if they intended to hire you, they got distracted. For whatever reason, they never get around to it. Without another round of advertising, they may forget how to contact you. Crazy as it sounds, someone can Google you, find your website, call you, and come to your office. But three weeks later, a Google algorithm update keeps them from finding you again.

That's why a lot of ecommerce advertisers invest in remarketing. Imagine you're shopping online for a toaster, but you leave the website before buying. All of a sudden, ads for that toaster are everywhere you go online—*that's* remarketing. If you added that toaster to your shopping cart but didn't check out, you trigger an abandoned cart sequence. That's why you get an email saying, *"You left an item in your cart. Act fast if you still want it!"* Advertisers know that a certain percentage of people who otherwise wouldn't have completed their purchase will come back and buy.

This kind of follow up matters now more than ever. In marketing, we used to have the Rule of Three—it took three touches on average before you associated a brand with the product they sold. In the internet age, the ocean is so bloody and competitive, studies suggest it takes more than *twenty-eight* touches. But if you do make that brand-product connection, you enjoy coveted "top of mind awareness" (TOMA). TOMA is how quickly a brand or a product comes to a consumer's mind.

When you think athletic shoes, who comes to mind? Nike.

When you think beer? Budweiser.

Facial tissues? Kleenex.

Soda? Coca-Cola.

Bandages? Band-Aid.

Like these big brands, some lawyers spend millions on ads to get those twenty-eight valuable touches and create TOMA.

For example, who comes to mind when you think criminal defense? You think of O.J. Simpson's defender, Johnnie Cochran.

What about women's rights attorneys? Gloria Allred.

Personal injury? If you're on the east coast of the United States, John Morgan of Morgan & Morgan. If you're in the midwest, maybe it's Doug Mann of Dyer Garofalo Mann & Schultz. If you're a west coaster, maybe Robert Reeves is top of mind.

Cochran and Allred didn't spend a lot of money. They did something significant instead. You can take on the case of a lifetime, but how often do those come along? And I'm obviously not going to ask new lawyers like Renee to spend millions and millions of dollars to create top of mind awareness. Because she didn't have to. Neither do you.

The New Way to Get Law Clients: Stop Talking, Start Giving

Like Renee, if you provide value *first*, you create a recognizable brand and top of mind awareness *without* spending millions on ads. And you'll never have to worry about somebody coming in, leaving, and never calling again. I get it—this is very different from anything you've ever heard of or read before. Your competition is all about big egos and big billboards.

"I'm a lawyer. I'm here for you. Call me."

That's the old way of doing things. And that's what most lawyers still do. They think they can just say, "Need legal help? Hire me!" and they'll get clients. It's kind of like opening a restaurant and expecting people to walk in off the street and fill the tables. When has that ever worked?

What I'm giving you is a new way to get more law clients so you *don't have to compete*. All you have to do is stop talking about yourself all the time and start giving prospective clients what they want. Forget the old way of doing things. If you want to be the go-to legal expert in your market, do what other lawyers don't— provide a lot of value *before* the client hires you. I agree with Tony Robbins:

> I discovered a long time ago that if I helped enough people get what they wanted, I would always get what I wanted and I would never have to worry.[1]

It's counterintuitive, but value-first works. If we help others get everything they want, we'll get everything we want, too. That's why I've been successful. I publish content every day on social media and push it out to my email list because I want to help lawyers grow their firms. I know it'll come back to me tenfold. Because I provide value before asking for anything in return, I can take Fridays off and live the life I want.

If you're skeptical, think about the last time you went to the food court at a mall. Why is there always a line at the Asian restaurants and not so much of a line at the other places? Because they've got employees out in the food court handing out free samples. People flock over there, enjoy the samples, and then become customers. People get value upfront, like what they taste, and line up to pay for a meal. The ones that provide value upfront are the ones that people buy from. If the other places were smart, they'd give out samples too. But just like your competition, they're stuck in the old way of doing business.

Sam's Club uses the same strategy. My kids love Sam's Club because they know they're going to get free samples. And I know that something they sample is going to end up in our cart. I can only resist my kids so much, after all.

"Fine, we'll get the marshmallows."

That wouldn't happen if they didn't provide value upfront. My kids aren't searching the aisles reading labels, waiting for the word "marshmallow" to jump out at them. They try a sample, and we're instantly a customer. This exact same strategy can work for you. After all, you're selling to the same consumers who eat at the Japanese food court restaurant and shop at Sam's Club. The same psychology applies. Give value, get clients. It's that simple. Just because you can't offer coupons like restaurants can—"Buy One Divorce, Get One Free!"—doesn't mean you can't *market* like them.

I'm not suggesting you advertise (or even offer) *pro bono* services. Follow Renee's lead—offer a *sample* of your work by solving a small minor problem. This builds goodwill. Just because you answered their question doesn't mean they no longer need a lawyer. What disgruntled wife says to a family lawyer, "Thanks for answering my questions about a dissolution. I'll take it from here!"? The act of *answering* her questions is going to prove to her how much she needs your services!

As another example, I know a personal injury lawyer who meets many people who are afraid of going to court.

"I don't want to go to court," they admit. "I'm not the litigious type. I don't want to get up there and sue people."

So this attorney sits down with them and explains, "Actually, you *don't* have to go to court. Here are all of your options, as well as the pros and cons of each." Who is the client going to hire?

Another personal injury lawyer I know wants to become the go-to attorney for traumatic brain injury (TBI) clients. While other law firms in town brag about huge settlements, this lawyer understands TBI victims. They just want to cover medical expenses and provide for their families. So he created a free step by step guide to set up a crowdfunding campaign to help cover medical bills in the short term. And the best part is, once the lawyer provides this value one time, he can do it over and over again with other potential clients without any additional work. Pure value. No pitches. No spamming.

Your value is directly proportional to what you give. Think about it. If your spouse gives and gives and gives, and you don't give anything, you don't have much value to your spouse. They're probably going to start looking for a new spouse soon!

When someone hires you, it's not because of the plaques on your wall. They hire you because the *value* of hiring you exceeds the *price* of hiring you. People hire you because of the benefits they receive by hiring you—what you can do for them, what value you can give to them. Keep that at the forefront of all your marketing endeavors, and marketing is *easy*. All you have to worry about is providing value, providing value, providing value.

Invest a little time (not tons of money) to provide value, and you'll become the most relevant lawyer your prospects know. People will start to see you as a credible, trustworthy authority. If you're a personal injury attorney, and you've been practicing for any period of time, you're most likely an expert. You can't call yourself an expert or a specialist, but you can easily be *perceived* as both. You'll decommoditize yourself. You'll separate yourself from other attorneys in town who charge a high hourly rate to answer basic questions.

That's the power of free samples. You'll create so much goodwill that by the time you *do* make an offer, your potential clients will be more than ready to bite. And like Renee, it's not just one or two people. It's several. Because when you provide as much value as you can for free, your online following grows organically. The public recognizes you as a high value source, and people share your website, your content, and your messages all over the internet.

And Now, a Word from the President

If the 2016 Presidential Election taught us anything, it's that the person who makes the most noise gets the most attention. Love him or hate him, Donald Trump can teach lawyers how to market themselves without outspending competitors. The Democratic National Committee and Hillary Clinton presidential campaign outspent Trump and the Republicans by a two-to-one margin. Yet Trump created *more* brand awareness and top of mind recognition through earned media. Earned media is the value of media coverage received that wasn't bought. For example, if one video viewer is worth $0.50, and the video goes viral with five million views, the ad got $2.5 million worth of earned media.

> From July 2015 to October 2016, Donald Trump received *five billion dollars'* worth of free media coverage.[2] Why? Experts like Dan Henry point out that he made more noise than anyone else. More noise, more coverage; more coverage, even more noise! As a result, we've now got President Trump.

If we can learn anything from history, it's that creating noise leads to success. I'm not saying *you* need to be outrageous or controversial. You're not trying to win an election, you just want more clients. In an election, all the other candidates are actively trying to win votes. But as a lawyer, most of your competition is asleep at the wheel. They're running one-off ads about their legal services and wondering where the clients are.

Make a little noise, and people give you a *lot* of attention. Noise doesn't have to be obnoxious, controversial, or polarizing like a campaign. Your noise is your free value. Think useful information, legal support, and helpful answers that your competitors charge by the hour to provide.

That's why it's important to keep staying on people's radar without being aggressive or salesy about it. Don't end every answer with a sales pitch. Most people are not ready to contact you on the first touch. Lawyers contact me after the twentieth, thirtieth, or even fortieth touch with my brand. Long after I started proving my authority.

Don't brag about the value you're providing. People are smart. They'll get it. Take Jerry Seinfeld. He never once says, "I'm going to tell you a joke, and you're going to laugh your butt off." He just tells the joke!

In the same way, if you're a DUI attorney and you put a lot of free content out there about DUIs and the law, people will make the connection. And when anyone needs you, they won't go to Google and search "DUI attorney near me." They'll seek you out *personally*, excluding all other lawyers from their legal search. Why? Because *you* are the authoritative figure who consistently provides value. When your audience needs a service you provide, you're the only option they consider. Even if your clients have a very poor opinion of lawyers generally (and let's face it, most of them do) they'll trust and respect you.

I know this because I'm in a similar position. Lawyers do *not* like marketing companies. They're sick of getting inundated with marketing materials promising the world. But after I give away marketing tutorials, advertising ideas, and SEO hacks, ten to fifteen lawyers contact me every single week. My agency is full, but it's still interesting to see how I've gone from the guy selling to the one being sold to. In fact, I recently I did an experiment in my online group, Lawyer Marketing. I asked members a question. Check out this screenshot to see my quick survey.

As expected, I got a ton of negative responses. Technically, I *am* an Internet Marketing Specialist and an SEO Expert. All of the lawyers in that comments feed think they're spammy. But I've differentiated myself. I've proven my authority and provided a ton of value. I've separated myself from the pack. Lawyers don't even think of me as a typical Internet Marketing Specialist or an SEO Expert. Imagine if I ran ads to lawyers with headlines like, "Hire me to do your law firm's SEO," or "Let me build you a website." *Nobody* would contact me!

The same goes for your legal services. Provide value, and you protect your brand from negative perceptions or lawyer stereotypes. You're different from *any* lawyer they've seen before. That's how every lawyer should market their services, but very few do. That means right now—not next month, not next year—is the ideal time to start providing your value. Put it off, and you risk another DUI lawyer or personal injury lawyer or criminal defense lawyer providing value *first*. Karen Lamb says:

A year from now you may wish you had started today.[3]

I call BS on that. A year from now, you will *absolutely* wish you started today. I'm doing well, and I wish I'd started *two* years ago. Now, like I said, you don't need to see how many legal services you can provide to the public *pro bono*. Solve *small* problems. Offer free *samples*.

Remember, as an attorney, your job has a big impact on people's lives. Your expertise is a "superpower," even if it doesn't seem like a big deal to you. After all, you've been a family law attorney or an employment attorney for so long now. The information you picked up in law school and gained through experience feels like old news.

Law comes naturally to you, but even a tiny percentage of your knowledge is *insanely* valuable to somebody in need of your services. You may know all the rules surrounding DUIs, like when a police officer can or can't take a Blood Alcohol Concentration test. Somebody who was just arrested for DUI doesn't know any of that. That person is terrified of what could happen in the next few weeks, and they need an attorney. They have so many questions, and if you can provide those answers, that alone is extremely valuable— valuable enough to hire you or retain you.

But what if I'm not the best attorney in town? Or the most experienced? You might be thinking. That negative inner voice doesn't matter. Besides, you've probably gone on Google, looked up law firms in your area, and thought, *Really? THEY are number one in the rankings?* or, *That guy's horrible. He doesn't even handle his own cases.*

At the end of the day, no law client cares how big you are. As long as you help them achieve the outcome they want, they won't even care if you work out of your friend's bedroom. People care about what you can do *for them*. The lawyer who *proves* what their firm can do before asking for the sale *wins*. I disagree with the famous Woody Allen quote:

Eighty percent of success is showing up.[4]

I say it accounts for *ninety-five* percent of success. Like I said, there's no competition to provide the most value. Position yourself as a helpful authority who helps people navigate the legal system. You're well on your way to becoming the next Johnnie Cochran, Gloria Allred, or John Morgan without landing the case of a lifetime or spending millions on ads.

If a twenty-something fresh out of law school can build her dream law firm by providing value first, *so can you*. In the coming chapters, you'll discover the step by step tactics I've taught thousands of lawyers around the world. Providing value starts with solutions to small problems, but it doesn't end there. Add value wherever you can, from first touch to first call to first case and beyond. You'll identify a niche, build a community, and provide value. You'll get ideal retainer clients who refer you to family, friends, and the world. It's a virtuous cycle. Provide value without expecting to get anything back, and I promise you, it *will* come back to you tenfold. In the words of the President...

Believe me!

Chapter 2
The Riches Are In the Niches

"The Best Money I've Ever Spent on Marketing."

Five years ago, a lawyer paid me $30,000 to market his law firm. I knew exactly what I was doing. So I thought.

I'd recently teamed up with the national sales director of one of the largest attorney marketing agencies. This new client marked our first sale together—and my first time working with a law firm. Previously, I worked with gyms, restaurants, dentists—all local businesses. Every time we ran a coupon campaign or published a two-for-one special on social media, my clients couldn't keep up with the new business.

How hard could marketing a law firm be? I thought. *I can't do coupons, but surely what works for every other business will work with law firms.*

Like I did for other clients, I wrote blog articles about the lawyer's services, created social media posts promoting his blog, and advertised those posts on a few bucks a day. The classic hope and pray method—hope and pray somebody sees the ad once and immediately calls the lawyer. Then run the ad over, and over, and over, reaching more and more people. Nobody answered my prayers.

We'd already cashed our client's check, but all I had to show for it were several likes, a few comments, and some traffic. No cases, no clients.

What if I can't turn this around? What if he asks for...a refund?! We're SCREWED.

Adding to the stress of my client's failing marketing campaign, my wife gave birth. Now I had a family to provide for and a company selling something that didn't work. Perfect.

In a panic, I threw money at the problem. I repurposed my services fee into PPC ads. But at $150 to $200 a click, I depleted my own salary as fast as my wife burned through her maternity leave. The Monday after Thanksgiving, she dropped our infant daughter off at daycare so she could go back to work.

I'm supposed to be the man of the house—the provider. And I'm letting everybody down. My family... My client... My new business partner...

By the end of the holiday season, I'd lost thirty pounds. I felt like we were ripping this guy off—albeit unintentionally.

I can't keep doing this. If he asks for his money back, what am I going to say? I've already spent it all on tactics that didn't work!

Three months into this insanity, I decided to relearn marketing. Well, what I *thought* was marketing. I gave Search Engine Optimization (SEO) a shot first. After all, I'd gotten emails over, and over, and over claiming, "We guarantee you the number one spot on Google." How hard could it be?

Granted, I didn't know much about SEO at the time. I climbed this learning curve by reading SEO articles and taking web development courses during the day. At night, I stayed up and implemented the day's lessons for my client. Apparently, humans can go on four hours of sleep for *weeks* at a time.

The entire time I studied SEO and optimized my client's website, I kept bumping into the same roadblock. *Google is always changing.* Five hundred major updates a year means most of the SEO advice I found was either outdated or just plain wrong. But test, after test, after test, I cracked the SEO code. I got my client to number one on Google, and the leads *finally* came.

Happy client, happy life.

He recorded a testimonial video and referred other attorneys to me. My business venture with the now ex-national sales director took off to the point I had to *stop* taking on new clients. More importantly, my wife quit her job to stay home with our daughter. I also got a good night's sleep. Finally.

Everything went great with that attorney and other new clients. But Google's algorithm updates kept coming. My clients all did well on Google, but I had *zero* control over their traffic. This business felt like throwing darts at a moving board.

What happens if Google makes a major update one day that changes everything? All the traffic, all the leads, gone. I had an epiphany. *It's time to try something else.*

SEO was a tough game because I competed against the smartest thing ever created—Google. Google uses a machine-learning artificial intelligence system called RankBrain. The software is so good at ranking websites, the engineers who developed it *don't even know how it ranks websites anymore!* The AI is always learning and always changing, and it's only going to stay that way. Google has a *lot* of money to play with. Google makes $2378.23 *per second*.[1] That's $8.5 million *every single hour*. The vast majority of this revenue comes from ads. Of course, nobody would use Google if *all* they offered was advertising. They have to have organic search, so SEO isn't dead. It *did* work, and it *was* worth it. Still, it's getting harder and harder to hold that first page prime real estate.

I didn't want my clients—or my family—putting all of our eggs in one basket. As with the social media ads, I hoped and prayed *something* else would work to keep my clients happy and the leads a-plenty.

Then one day during a phone meeting with a criminal defense lawyer out of Dallas, Texas, I had an idea.

"Andy, I really need your help," he said. "I'm getting evicted from my office this week if I don't get at least one client so I can pay the rent. Over my thirty-year career, I've tried everything."

I'd just built and launched his website, but SEO takes time—too much time for this guy to wait.

"Well, you primarily defend nurses in danger of having their licenses revoked, right?" I said. "So what if, instead of running ads talking about *you* and *your* criminal defense law firm, we talk about nurses?"

"Go on."

"We run ads targeting Dallas nurses, letting them know they have a local champion who specializes in nursing board license defense. We can't use the word 'specialize.' Maybe 'offers services in...' But they'll make the connection."

He gave me the go-ahead, and I scrambled. I worked all night on the radically different marketing strategy. How could I *not*? No stopping, no sleep. By the end of the week, he had several new clients—enough new business to pay the rent. All nurses who needed legal representation. Mind: blown.

"The clients are the exact type of client I'm looking for," he told me on our next call. "The best money I've *ever* spent on marketing."

I did it. After all my blood, sweat, and tears spent figuring out the right way to market a law firm...*I did it*.

Then came the hard part.

How do I replicate this attorney's results?

When I thought about the nurse niche ad, the answer hit me like a ton of bricks.

It's not the ad, it's the NICHE! The NICHE is the secret!

Why did the nursing license defense ad work better than everything else he'd tried in the last thirty years? Because he **added value**. The ad linked to a blog article which answered the top concerns of nurses facing suspension. With a single ad, my client proved to nurses that someone out there "got" them and their specific situation. It wasn't enough to be a generic legal expert. My client was perceived as *the legal expert for nurses facing license suspension*. He provided value by solving small problems. Help people solve a small problem, and they will hire you for the big problem.

It turns out that *specific* expertise in the relevant legal field is the number one criteria people use to choose an attorney.[2] Even more than recommendations from friends and family, more than location, and more than a sense of trustworthiness. In other words, the legal consumer's first concern is, *I need an expert but I don't know who to choose*. So the first way to provide value in the attorney-client relationship is to decide *who* you're going to provide value to. Then position yourself as their best choice. Obviously, you don't *just* want people to recognize your expertise. You want their case. But half of the persuasion battle is the public's attention.

That's exactly why the Dallas attorney's ad worked. He showed a specific niche he could help their specific situation, and they jumped at the opportunity. Fast forward to today, and I try to get every lawyer I work with to target a niche.

I don't know who came up with it first, but they were right when they said, "The riches are in the niches." As a lawyer, the more niche you can get, the better off you are. Look at my business. I focus on marketing for lawyers. Not lawyers plus dentists, real estate agents, and accountants. Become the absolute king (or queen) in one niche. Don't dabble. Be a master of one, not a master of none.

How to Provide Value (By Picking the Right Niche)

A personal injury lawyer client of mine in Georgia targets the Atlanta motorcycle accident niche. He doesn't officially "specialize" in motorcycle accidents, but he has chosen that niche to build credibility and add value. Now that he's the authority, he receives several invitations a month to speak at biker events!

Just because he targets the biker niche doesn't mean he *only* gets motorcyclist cases. For example, a member of his group reached out to him for a nursing home abuse case. He's *the* personal injury law expert. Who else would they turn to for legal representation? Some schmuck in the Yellow Pages?

Plus, new clients didn't just come from his group. Bikers ride in groups of forty or fifty. Even if only *one* person is in my client's group, he is connected to *all* of those riders. In fact, someone in the group referred a friend with a high-profile wrongful death lawsuit. My client provided so much value to the group, he turned them into evangelists for his firm.

How awesome would it be if people told *everyone* they knew about you because they viewed you as the authority in your niche? That's happening to lawyers all over the world who follow this strategy, and it can happen to you as well. That doesn't mean *you* should target suspended nurses and injured motorcyclists. These are examples. Other PI niches include, but are certainly not limited to construction workers, Baby Boomers (nursing home abuse), and family of brain injury victims. I have another client who targets parents of children injured on playgrounds. The possibilities are endless.

Criminal defense lawyers can go beyond DUIs. Think college students, young professionals, or single working mothers with DUIs. Or focus on the families of people facing alcohol or drug addiction. Or Second Amendment proponents. Simply put, you're reverse-engineering your ideal clients, those who make up your niche. When you think about people who need your legal services, who needs a lawyer *more than the average person*? For example, a staggering *one in five* college students admits to driving drunk.[3] If you're a criminal defense lawyer, college students with DUIs may be the best niche for you. Often, college kids' parents foot the bill—another potential niche for you.

Whatever your niche, stick with it and become the authority. Do this, and you add *incredible* value. You're helping potential clients skip the painstaking lawyer research process and go straight to the expert—*you*.

Think about how much time you spent researching the last smart product you bought. A smartphone, a TV, a wireless speaker. Probably at least a few hours. You read reviews, compared features, and hunted around for the best price. Now, double or triple that time researching (and stressing) for a single mom about to lose her nursing license. She's scouring the internet for legal advice, calling every law firm on the first page of Google, and crying over her career ending. All while pretending everything is okay so her kids don't worry. Then along comes an expert in nursing board license defense, and she sees a light at the end of the tunnel. The attorney is providing answers to her problems, and she hasn't even met him yet.

This niche strategy works for all types of lawyers. Family lawyers. Business lawyers. Immigration lawyers. Employment lawyers. Real estate lawyers. Bankruptcy lawyers. Estate planning lawyers. Probate lawyers. Workers comp lawyers. IP lawyers and more.

Family law attorneys can target domestic violence, fathers, mothers, or just parents in general. Or you could focus on grandparents raising their grandchildren, or single parents of adopted children. Business lawyers could go after Amazon sellers, restaurant owners, or freelancers. Gig economy workers might not realize what liabilities come with self-employment. Immigration attorneys can become the authority for Russians who live in Fresno or Germans who live in San Diego. You could target foreign investors or human resources departments at companies with H1B workers. Employment lawyers could target employees of specific businesses, like Disney or Fedex. For estate planning, target business owners who may not realize that if they die, their families are screwed. You can also focus on younger parents who have no idea that estate planning is not just for old, rich people. If you've got a house and at least one kid, estate planning is for you. Bankruptcy lawyers could target millennials who need debt relief or credit repair. Tax attorneys can become the expert in a specific industry or profession. Airline pilots or ecommerce retailers facing IRS audits, for example. Intellectual property lawyers can focus on inventors, writers, freelancers. Any creative people who need legal protection, basically.

This is just a short list of examples. Be creative. Don't feel like just because a niche doesn't appear in this book, it isn't a good one. With all the potential niches your law firm *could* target, which should you choose?

First of all, a good niche requires *passion*. Do you personally have more empathy for a specific type of client over another? Do other people share your passion? I know several family law attorneys who are big believers in the role a father plays in his children's lives. Who do you think they target? The men's rights and father's rights niche.

Another criteria for a good niche is impact—both personal and financial. The father's rights niche absolutely impacts people's lives. Kids need quality, unsupervised time with fathers who love them.

Of course, your niche must be able to *afford* you. Almost every lawyer I've ever met has a non-paying client horror story. That type of client is the opposite of a good niche. Don't go there again. The first rule of the niche strategy is to *never* sell things to broke people.

And just as you'll know who *isn't* a good niche, you'll also want to be super clear on the right one. The more specific, the better. Remember, the Dallas criminal defense attorney didn't niche down to nurses generally. He targets nurses *facing license suspension*. And the Atlanta personal injury lawyer doesn't niche down to traffic accidents. He targets *motorcyclists* because they are ten times more likely to suffer injuries than other motorists.[4]

A great way to find out if you've picked the right niche is if communities already exist. A good way to check is to go to Facebook, search for groups, and see what you find.

For example, brain injury support groups on social media have thousands of members. Imagine you're a personal injury attorney in Tallahassee. You create a Tallahassee Brain Injury Support Group. You target people who may have brain injuries, or family of people who have brain injuries. (More on groups in Chapter 5.)

Let's say you get just five new people per day. That's almost 2,000 per year, or nearly 10,000 over the next five years. And all of these people have a loved one or a family member with a brain injury. A lot of them are going to have questions, and at least a handful of members are going to need an attorney. What's going to happen? As this group continues to be active, it's going to start growing. People join organically. Somebody who was just in a car accident a month ago has a mother who is active on social media. She's been researching brain injuries and the long-term consequences. All of a sudden, she sees your niche group—Tallahassee Brain Injury Support Group—or your accompanying Youtube channel (More on video in Chapter 6). Why in the world *wouldn't* she click? To that grieving mother—and thousands of others—you're *the* authority. Your niche is desperate for accurate information...and for help.

Now, five new people in your group per day may not seem like many, but over time, you build an incredibly profitable following. Once again, I agree with Tony Robbins.

> Most people overestimate what they can do in a year and they underestimate what they can do in two or three decades.[5]

Like every value-first strategy in this book, a niche is not a get rich quick scheme. I don't believe in gimmicks. We've all gotten those emails promising tons of leads overnight. When I began my law firm marketing journey, I just wanted to figure out how to get consistent leads for my clients. I needed a reliable, predictable, competition-free process. I discovered the first step to providing free value—**pick the right niche**.

Once you have a niche, you're the expert trusted by *thousands*. And you're providing value because *you* are the legal expert for their specific situation. No worrying, no time wasted researching, no getting scammed by your sleazy competitor.

But before you do ANYTHING else (like start a group), you have to give your niche—and all potential clients—a low-friction path to become clients. And how do you do *that*? It's simple—*ask them*.

Chapter 3
Cheeseburgers or Broccoli?

What No Law School Teaches

Do you know the secret to marketing anything in the world? Figure out what people want and give it to them. That's it. That's the secret. Once you figure out what people want, marketing your law firm becomes the easiest thing you've ever done.

How can I be so confident? Because people buy what they *want*, not what they *need*. Do I *need* a cheeseburger? No, I *need* to eat the broccoli, but I order a hamburger off the menu because that's what I want.

Market your law firm *with* human nature, not against it. Your job is to sell people what they want, not what they need. No law school teaches this. So it's not your fault you've never heard this before. Not even marketing *agencies* get this. Over-complicate your marketing, and it doesn't work. If you don't figure out what people want *first*, no number of $200 per-click ads can save you.

A lot of lawyers create free legal guides, write blog posts, and print pamphlets about "what people need to know." That's not how our brains work. We humans buy what we want, read what we want, eat what we want, and watch what we want— not what we need. That includes legal services like yours and marketing services like mine.

Seriously, why would I talk about anything other than what lawyers want? If I want lawyers to hire my marketing firm, why would I talk about my experience? All the lawyer cares about is getting clients. They don't care about how much experience I have. They care about what they're going to *get out of hiring me*.

It's the same thing with your clients. They only care about what you can do for them—the end result. They don't care about your experience or your background. That said, actually figuring out what people—*your* people—really want isn't up to your gut. Base your marketing on facts and data, not just what you *think* people want. Fortunately, even if you just passed the bar last week, you already have access to the data you need.

For example, if you're a divorce attorney, figure out what your divorce clients want, then find more people like them. If you can figure out what their desires are and what their fears are, *any* marketing you do *will* work. Now, notice I bring up fears, too. The average person doesn't just have wants, they also have don't-wants. For example, if you're a bankruptcy attorney, your clients have a *lot* to be afraid of.

Imagine everything happening in a bankruptcy client's head.

Am I going to lose my house? And my car? I can't afford an attorney. But I need one. What if I can't pay him? What then? I am SCREWED.

This client has many fears, but the biggest result they *want* is debt resolution.

I want to get out of debt. I HAVE to get out of debt. These bills are KILLING me. I can't take one more bill collector call. If I could just get my head above water...

However, getting out of debt may not be *all* they want. Maybe they're concerned about buying a house. Maybe their credit it relevant to their job. Maybe they want to go back to school and need to free up part of their income from bills. Whatever your clients want, *talk about it.*

If you're a bankruptcy lawyer, all of your messaging should be about giving people what they want—peace of mind, repaired credit, and no more bill collectors. Whatever that biggest desire is, lead with that. They don't care that you have twenty-five years of experience or that you're board-certified. Yes, they *need* an experienced, certified attorney, but nowhere in their desires or fears does that show up. Change your messaging to what people want (and don't want), and you'll get and keep attention.

It's the same with child custody law. Many single or divorced fathers fear losing custody of their kids.

What if I don't get to see my kids at all? What if they forget me? The courts never rule in dads' favor.

If your niche is divorced fathers struggling with custody, don't talk about your legal expertise. *Show* your expertise by talking about what they want, and what they don't want. In fact, my favorite messaging formula is "how to get what you want without that thing you're afraid of." (More on this later.)

For now, you want to nail your niche's wants and don't-wants— their desires and their fears. Otherwise, your messaging backfires. You come off sounding like a sleazy late-night infomercial. That means no guesses. If I want lawyers eating out of the palm of my marketing hand, I have to ask my niche questions, then create content based on their answers. In my case, it's as simple as posting a question in my social media group, Lawyer Marketing.

Andy Stickel
🛡 **Admin** · March 17

•••

I've been getting a ton of messages on Facebook from some members of this group asking how to get more clients from social media.

I already put out a free cheat sheet, but I'm thinking of doing a free live video training covering this subject.

Would anyone be interested in this?

👍 James Bendell, Joe Michelotti and 17 others   13 Comments

One hour later, several comments. All, "Yes." I messaged each person a survey with follow up questions.

Do you want to learn to get more law clients using social media?

Have you already started using social media to generate clients?

What is your #1 goal when it comes to using social media to get clients?

What is the #1 roadblock that stands in your way of this goal? Why haven't you started? What is your obstacle?

What is the #1 thing you want to learn regarding using social media to get more law clients?

What is your #1 fear you want to avoid at all costs?

I didn't guess—I asked. I found out that lawyers *want* to get more clients from social media. And I found out that they're *afraid* of losing time, losing money, and getting screwed by a marketing company. (Sound familiar?) Good thing I asked. I fully expected lawyers to want help building their own websites and mastering SEO. Not the case.

You may be ninety-nine percent certain what your niche wants. But is it worth the risk of guessing? It sure wasn't for me. Ask your niche what they want (and don't) to confirm you're correct. How would you feel if, six or eight weeks down the road, you find out you're wrong after you've done all this work?

Your First Campaign—Ask

Market research expert Ryan Levesque, author of *Ask: The Counterintuitive Online Formula to Discover Exactly What Your Customers Want to Buy...Create a Mass of Raving Fans...and Take Any Business to the Next Level*, calls the ask-don't-guess approach an Ask Campaign.

For your Ask Campaign, make sure you're talking to people who fit your ideal client profile—your niche. For example, if you're trying to target fathers, don't ask your wife what she thinks a father's biggest divorce fears are. She'll be wrong, and she may even get suspicious!

When you do ask your niche about their desires and fears, don't treat your conversation like an interview. And it doesn't have to feel "official" or awkward. You can approach the topic casually. Say, "I'm going to put out a free resource, and I want to make sure I cover all the topics you're interested in so it's as helpful as possible."

Your first Ask Campaign questions are for vetting purposes only.

Do you want to learn more about _____?

For example, I would ask lawyers, "Do you want to learn more about marketing your law firm on social media?"

I want people *not* in my niche to self-identify. Don't care to learn more? Great! I can ignore the rest of your answers.

You also want to get an idea of where people are in the process. For example, let's say you're a family law attorney. You could ask, "Are you interested in learning more about how to get divorced without losing custody of your children?" (See how I include the desire *and* the fear?)

If people say, "Yes," then ask, "Have you already started the divorce process?" This quick follow up tells you how relevant their overall feedback will be. The closer a person is to your ideal client profile, the more stock you should put in their answers. From there, ask broad, easy questions before you dig deep into your niche's psyche.

What is your number one question about _____?

For your survey, your question might read like one of these.

What is your number one question about filing for bankruptcy?

What is your number one question about divorce?

What is your number one question about dealing with a brain injury?

What's your number one question about dealing with the IRS?

Ask and listen. Take copious notes. If you're sending out a text-based survey, compile all your answers in a single working document. You'll need quick, easy access to these later—trust me. Next, prod people to get specific.

What is your main goal regarding _____?

What's the number one thing you'd like to learn regarding _____?

What else would you like to learn?

Their answers tell you what the core focus of your messaging should be—specifically, the messaging around your *bait*. (More on that later, too.) And last of all (but most important), figure out what your niche fears.

What is the number one thing about _____ you want to avoid at all costs?

For example, family law attorneys could ask, "What is the number one thing about getting a divorce you want to avoid at all costs?"

To wrap up your survey or interview, put yourself in position to follow up—and potentially turn that person into a client.

What is your email address so I can send you the free resource when it's ready?

Again, you probably think you know what your niche would say word for word. In that case, just confirm your suspicions. Wouldn't it be great to not have to worry if you're targeting the right people or if you're giving them what they actually want?

Once you've talked to a minimum of ten people, you have enough data to call your Ask Campaign a success. To find these ten people, you don't have to post on social media like I did. Use the resources you already have. I had a group, so I asked my group. You can call friends and family in the niche you're targeting and offer to buy them coffee.

If you're an estate planning attorney, call up a family friend and say, "I'm an attorney, as you know. You have kids. You have a business. Have you ever thought about an estate plan? I'm not trying to sell you anything. I'm just trying to put out free resources, so I'm trying to get into the heads of people who might be a good client. So, what are some of the things you're thinking about with estate planning? Are you *even thinking* about estate planning?"

If you have past clients, reach out and say, "I'm trying to create a free resource that's going to help people who were in your position before you came to me. What were some of your fears? What was your number one question about brain injuries?"

Insert your questions into casual conversation like this, and you come across as non-threatening. You're getting their advice—not interviewing them. You can also ask current clients. If you're already speaking with a client, bring it up on the spot. Say, "I'm trying to put together a free resource for people who might need help. Obviously, you've been going through this, so you're getting a lot of your questions answered. But there's a lot of people out there just like you who have a ton of questions. They don't know where to start, so I'm trying to put a resource together to help them out. Before we started, what was your number one question about divorce?"

If you don't have your own social media group, look up existing ones. If you want to create a resource for families of the drug-addicted, join addiction support groups online. Introduce yourself and ask, "I'm putting out a free resource, and I wanted to find out how to make it super helpful. If you could ask a criminal defense attorney about crimes related to addiction, what would your number one question be? Answer in the comments below."

Just be careful how you phrase the question. Don't jam *every* question from your Ask Campaign into your post. Many group administrators are very sensitive to spam. Act like you're trying to get something out of the group without adding value, and you'll get banned. If possible, reach out to one of the admins beforehand for approval. If you pulled a Renee and became the go-to legal authority in the group, expect a resounding, "YES!"

Groups in your niche aren't only on social media. If you're struggling to score ten interviews, search for online message boards and forums. Contact the moderators, and ask permission to post your question. I've seen lawyers do this, and the moderator posts on their behalf! That gives the question a lot more authority, so more people answer. Offer to share either the email addresses you collect or the survey answers with moderators. Another reason to help you connect with their members!

Still need people? Contact local organizations who also serve your niche. You could reach out to brain injury foundations, addiction support foundations, whatever your niche is. Look up someone in their public relations or community outreach department, then call them and say, "I'm an attorney. I'm trying to create a free resource to help families dealing with _____. I'm trying to make the resource as useful as possible. To do that, I want to find out more about these people's thoughts. What do they want? What do they fear? What are they worried about? What keeps them up at night?"

Established organizations—especially those who fundraise—already have the built-in audience you need. Offer to share your answers with them. Combine your request with a reasonable donation, and now you're *sponsoring* the survey. The organization will put your logo next to theirs, giving you even more credibility.

If all else fails, run ads on social media. Advertising an Ask Campaign is my least favorite method, but in case you and your niche live under separate rocks, ads are an option.

Give Value, Get Value

So, now you've asked. And your niche answered. Now what?

My first Ask Campaign inspired me to run a webinar training, create a multimedia masterclass, and write a book (this one). Your content doesn't have to be a webinar, a course, or a book, but it does have to be *bait*. Maybe it's a cheat sheet, a video, or a creative resource no other lawyer in your area offers (like a quiz). You're going to use this bait to gather leads, capture their email addresses, and bring them into your world.

I like quizzes because so few lawyers do them. For example, I developed a Diminished Value Recovery Quiz for a car accident attorney client. When someone starts the quiz, they first see an explanation of diminished value in plain English.

Did you know that you may be entitled to $3,000 to $5,000, depending on what your diminished value is?

Then they see Ask Campaign-style questions.

Do you still own the vehicle?

Was the accident your fault?

Were you injured?

If so, do you have an attorney?

Get creative. Decide on your bait type, and make the content as high value as possible. But make sure it's not a sales pitch. That's how you build trust in your niche and maintain your credibility. Don't just write a piece called, "Reasons You Need a Personal Injury

Attorney," or "Why You Need to Hire an Employment Lawyer." People aren't stupid. You have a bio. They can read. I *promise* you—they know they need an attorney.

When I put my own bait out there, I don't sell anything. I don't ruin my high value content with a line like "Hey, if you need help with your marketing, call me today! I'll give you a free website evaluation." You won't see me do that because *every other marketer already does*.

I call this content "bait" because it's not a freebie or a handout. Yes, you're *giving* value, but you're also *getting* value. You're catching leads. People who read your cheat sheet or watch your video have their guards down. Most people get advertised to nonstop. They're used to having marketers try to sell them over, and over, and over. So when they see a piece of high-value content *without* a sales pitch, they like you. You're refreshing.

You can get a free landing page template to use at www.getlawfirmclients.com/resources.
You'll also get a complete tutorial to set up your page.

Providing value is kind of like the dating game. Back in my single days when I hung out with friends at the bar, I'd always see guys hitting on girls. They tried so hard. It was pathetic. My strategy to meet women? Don't take—*give*. I didn't try to sell myself. I just provided value. I entertained. I was funny. Everyone felt at ease around me. And I did pretty well. Human nature doesn't change, no matter the setting. What works at the *bar*...works for the *Bar*.

How to Fish For Clients

Your bait is your first chance to provide value to your niche. That said, it has to be *attractive* bait. The reality is, most people who download cheat sheets and ebooks never even open them, much less read them. To get people to click, read, and yes, contact you, call out their desires and fears. (That's what your Ask Campaign was for, after all!) Then write a "click bait" title. A hook. An attention-grabber. Remember my favorite messaging formula—"how to get <what you want> without <that thing you're afraid of>"? It's called a how-to-without statement.

How to <desire> without <fear>.

If you follow this formula, you cannot miss. You won't find a better, cheaper, faster way to get a prospect's attention. And yes, I drink my own Kool-Aid. This book borrows the title of my cheat sheet (and webinar) that got my agency booked solid.

How to Get More Law Clients Using Social Media Without Losing Time and Money, Or Getting Screwed by a Marketing Company.

And look, it worked! Not only did you buy my book, *you're reading it right now.* See how easy marketing is? You ask people what they want and what they're afraid of, and you listen. Marketing doesn't have to be hard.

To create your click bait title, just drop the answers from your Ask Campaign into the formula.

How To Survive Bankruptcy Without Losing Your House.

How To Get Divorced Without Losing Custody of your Kids.

How To Get Bill Collectors To Stop Harassing You, Even If You Can't Afford To Pay Them Right Now.

Get creative. Try numbers.

3 Ways To Live In The United States Without Fear Of Deportation.

5 Ways Experienced Lawyers Beat DUI Charges and Keep Their Clients Out of Jail.

5 Things All Construction Workers Must Know About On-The-Job Injuries, Even If You've Never Been Injured.

14 Ways Children Benefit From Divorce.

Beating A DUI Charge: 3 Things You Must Know Whether You've Been Arrested Or Not.

Use curiosity.

3 Motorcycle Features That Could Save Your Life.

How Fathers Can Get Divorced While Actually Increasing the Amount of Time They Get to Spend with Their Kids.

3 Pieces of Intellectual Property You Didn't Even Know You Had.

Here's What <u>Definitively</u> Happens When You Die.......Without an Estate Plan.

Need more inspiration? Work real-life examples into your title.

How We Helped One Client Eliminate All IRS Penalties With One Email.

As long as you're not making specific claims that will get you in trouble, you can get as creative as you like. If your niche finds your bait tasty, they'll immediately bite. A personal injury lawyer client posted a free guide to cyclist legal rights, and an injured bicyclist posted a comment.

This no-cost guide shows you:

- ☑ Which Laws Protect Cyclists in Florida
- ☑ The Best Safety Equipment & Gear
- ☑ Tips For Avoiding Accidents
- ☑ What To Do If Injured by a Careless Driver

Download and review this guide before your next ride.

[Free Guide]: Legal Rights of Cyclists & How to Stay Safe

Download

👥 4,283 people **reached**

New ▾

 _____ _____ was knocked off my bike two weeks ago and am still in a lot of pain and swelling and discomfort. I was hit from the rear and didn't know anything until I woke up in the hospital. My bike is irreparable and the driver's insurance wants to offer patience. My helmet is cracked, my head hurts, left ankle swollen, shoulders, chest and back hurts. According to CT scans taken I have no broken bones, however , I'm having an MRI of the leg and ankle to conclude the former results. This accident was in Weston in Florida in the bike lane. She must have been on her phone or texting. My uniform was bright and my rear lights were flashing. It was about 6.23 pm.

Like · Reply · See Response · 6d 2

"But I Don't Want to Be Salesy.

Four years ago, a personal injury lawyer hired me to market his law firm. At the time, he and his one assistant worked out of a five hundred square-foot office. At first, he hesitated. He didn't want to get scammed or lose money on advertising that doesn't work. I had to convince him to hire me. Now, he oversees *twelve* attorneys in an *eight thousand* square foot office. All because I did a great job marketing his law firm. Recently, I suggested we implement the Ask Campaign strategy.

"I don't know about that whole 'click bait' thing," he told me. "I like the idea of giving people what they want, but I don't want to be salesy."

"I totally get it. Let me ask you something," I said. "When you and I first started, I had to sell you on hiring me, right?"

"Right."

"Do you think you're better off since you hired me?"

He looked around at his office. Thank you notes from clients framed on the walls. Awards everywhere. Upscale furniture and expensive art decorated the room.

"Absolutely."

"You do a good job for your clients, too," I said. "When you knock it out of the park, they're better off having you as their attorney than someone else."

"No disagreement there." He laughed.

"If you really believe that, then you have a *moral obligation* to do whatever you need to do to win them as clients. Don't let them make the mistake of hiring somebody else and getting inferior representation."

He nodded. Slowly.

"Should we do a cheat sheet or a live training video?"

I can't take full credit for convincing my client to launch his first Ask Campaign. That morning, I'd been reading Jay Abraham, the marketing consultant to billionaires.

> If you truly believe that what you have is useful and valuable to your clients, then you have a moral obligation to try to serve them in every way possible.[1]

I agree with him. Do you?

Seven Keys to Lure Those Leads

You now know what your niche wants. You're creating bait to give it to them. So...*how* do you give it to them?Once your cheat sheet, video, or quiz is ready, email everyone you interviewed. But don't stop there. Your bait is for your *entire* niche, not just the people you talked to during the Ask Campaign.

How did you find people to interview in the first place? Did you start a group, join a forum, or connect with a local organization? Did you run ads on social media? What worked to find *ten* people can work to find *ten thousand*.

Eventually, you're going to turn your niche into a community. That means you need as many email addresses as possible. But first, you need to provide value—your bait. To do that, you're not going to cold-pitch your bait to strangers one at a time. Create a landing page for your bait—a special page on your site where incoming traffic "lands." (More on *how* to drive traffic to your website later.)

Compared to your website home page, a landing page has a much, much higher chance of capturing the attention of potential leads. Yes, your home page has useful functions. It introduces your brand, reflects your values, and links to the other areas of your website. It encourages your visitors to explore rather than convert. *You want conversions.*

Your bait's landing page exists for one reason only—to get a response to your call to action. Keep the text short and simple, and get to the point. Make it *easy* for visitors to respond. Don't clutter the page with *anything* that doesn't encourage the visitor to respond.

There's one more thing you don't want cluttering your landing page—and this is vital. Never, never use a "slider" on your bait landing page. A typical "slider" starts with a dynamic photo across the top of the page with a phrase like "Fighting for Justice Since 2002." Then another picture "slides" across the previous one. Maybe it's you working at your desk with a line of text like, "Over $30 Million in Verdicts for Clients."

Why avoid sliders? Attention spans are short. Sliders don't convert well on mobile devices (how half of your niche sees your page) or *any* device for that matter.[2] I call sliders "conversion killers" because they split a visitor's attention. The eye is automatically drawn to moving text and moving pictures. The slider distracts from your message—that juicy piece of bait you worked so hard to craft. People already have zero attention spans. And now you're adding moving images *and* text? You may as well close the page for them. Whenever I replace a slider with a static image, conversions double instantly. Sites with abundant traffic—but few conversions— suddenly start producing conversions.

Now that what not to do is out of the way, I'm going to make your bait page easy to set up. To create your high-converting bait landing page, grab your free landing page template at www.getlawfirmclients.com/resources.
You'll also get a complete tutorial to set up your page.

Once your landing page visitors type in their email address, congratulations! You now own the number one most valuable asset in all of marketing. A recent survey found that email has a median return-on-investment of 122%.[3] That's more than *four times higher* than other marketing, including social media, direct mail, and paid search.

I use email strategically. To generate leads in a recent campaign, I started with bait (as you will). I created an ad on social media, which sent traffic to my landing page. People entered their email address and downloaded my cheat sheet. Once these people were on my email list, they started getting useful emails from me every day. And every email tells people to join my group, Lawyer Marketing.

Join my free Lawyer Marketing group for daily marketing tips.

Together, these digital assets—bait, landing page, emails, community allow me to generate leads *on-demand*. Over the next couple of chapters, you're not only going to learn how to create high-converting social media ads, but how to build a community, too.

For now, I *cannot emphasize enough* how important your bait is. Many lawyers try to get law clients on social media, but they waste time and money like you wouldn't believe. All because they missed the most important piece of the profit puzzle—the Ask Campaign.

Find out what your niche wants first. Then give it to them. And give it to them over, and over, and over. What do you have to lose by providing consistent value? Like Jay Abraham said:

> [Your] competitors couldn't market their way out of a paper bag.[4]

Give people what they want, and they will lead you out of that paper bag. Every. Single. Time.

Chapter 4
Finding Your Pond

Advertising to Fish

If you've ever been fishing, you know the essentials. Fishing pole, check. Bait for the fish, check. A nice quiet spot by the water, check. But if you forget one crucial thing, nobody's having a fish fry—*the fish*.

It's the same in marketing. I see so many lawyers spend hours and hours tweaking that one sentence in their cheat sheet. They go back and forth for days with a freelance graphic designer over the typeface. Then something about the color is off. Got to change that, too.

If all a fisherman does is hook and unhook bait from the lure until it's *just* right, but he never drops it in the water, guess what? That's one hungry fisherman. And what if the fish don't like the bait?

Back to getting more law clients—once you know what your niche wants, give it to them. To *lots* of them. No waiting, no hesitating, no holding back. Drop your line into the waters of the world wide web, and watch the leads swim your way. It's *almost* that simple. In the age of social media advertising, law firms can reach billions and billions of prospects on just a few dollars a day. But how many leads you get—and how many convert into clients—all depends on how you cast your line. Or, in this case, how you advertise your bait.

> **By this point in the book, I assume a few things: You've picked a niche. You've completed an Ask Campaign. You've created your bait and you've come up with an awesome clickbait title. You've published your bait landing page using my free template at www.getlawfirmclients.com/resources. And you've set up your email list. If you haven't yet completed those steps, put this book down and get to work! Next up, *collecting those emails.***

Lead generation and client creation on-demand means *you* are in control. Everyday people who find you on search engines are still valuable, but that's traffic you don't control. The people who click your social media ad and visit your landing page are traffic you *do* control. You can turn the traffic on and off whenever you like.

To get clicks, traffic, and then leads, we're not going to run ads for your *legal services*. We're going to run ads for your *bait* or for the solution your bait provides. For example, I run ads that have nothing to do with my law firm marketing services. Provide value—give first, receive second, remember? When lawyers who've never heard of me before see my ad, they see *something they want*. My cheat sheet.

How to Get More Law Clients Using Social Media Without Losing Time and Money or Getting SCREWED By a Marketing Company.

When lawyers click through the ad to my landing page, they can't just download and read. They share their email address and join my list. I've now converted this traffic from traffic I *control* to traffic I *own*—and that's the best traffic there is.

From my email list, I invite lawyers to my Lawyer Marketing group and email them high-value content every day. But without the driving force of effective social media video ads, they never even enter my world.

Did you notice something about that last sentence? Social media *video* ads. So, why video? First and foremost, they just work better. Social media powerhouses like Facebook prefer video content to posts, updates, and yes, ads with only text or images. Unlike static pictures, videos allow you to build rapport immediately with your audience. They get to see you. They get to hear your voice. They get to understand your personality with all of your quirks. (Nobody's perfect on camera. That's a good thing, because people don't want *perfect*—they want *authentic*.)

If you've ever watched my videos, you know my voice and my mannerisms. And you know that I say, "You know?" all the time. Sure, it can be annoying, but it's part of my personality. My audience identifies me by my quirks. The same goes for you. Video shows your niche—your future clients—that you're an actual person, not just a business. You build rapport. You express yourself. And you get your message across. Video is the icing on the cake to establish you as the authority. You can run an ad with your picture, but when someone actually listens to you talk, they feel like they *know* you. That's powerful.

Even though most Millennials (people in their thirties and younger) prefer to text, I still like talking on the phone or, even better, face to face. I can get my message across better when I talk to people. When you're doing video, people hear what you have to say. It's a lot easier (and faster) than reading. At the end of the day, people are lazy. They don't want homework.

But video is effortless. They don't have to think, they don't have to read, they don't even have to *see* the video. They can have it on in the background and just listen. Believe it or not, reading is work for a lot of people. If you create a video that gets your message across without making people work, they'll consume your content. Even if that content is an advertisement.

Bottom line, video simply works better. You evoke emotion. You connect with the audience. It's the best way to go. That said, video was very scary for me when I started. I felt self-conscious. I sat in front of my webcam shooting take after take thinking, *I hate this. My voice sounds terrible.*

But I wasn't as bad as I thought I was. I bet you aren't either. And to be totally honest with you, it doesn't matter! For me, creating videos is the absolute best advertising decision I have ever made. Video will absolutely change your life. If you can talk, you can record a video.

Eight Video Essentials

So, you're sold on video—but don't go pressing "Record" on your smartphone camera just yet. An ad campaign where you wing it is an ad campaign that loses money. All the videos I do for my clients are deliberate and fluff-free. Start with the **eight essential video elements** and work them into the script.

When I added the eight essential elements to my script writing process, my ad conversion rates *quadrupled*. Just like my marketing mentor Dan Henry promised they would! Results come down to psychology. Communicate the value of what you're offering, and people can't look away. The eight elements help you do that in every single video ad.

The first essential element of your video ad is **pattern interrupt**. That's how you interrupt whatever a person is doing and grab their attention. If people aren't paying attention, they're not stopping to watch your ad in the first place. Even if they do stop scrolling and watch for a few seconds, they won't stick around long enough to understand your message. And they sure won't click your ad, visit your landing page, and join your email list. My favorite way to get attention with a video ad is a giant red bar.

Maybe you don't like red. Just pick a vibrant color that people can't miss. In the bar, call out your niche and their desire. You can even use unique images and controversial phrases.

Hey parents, want to spend more time with your kids?

Got a DUI? Want to stay out of jail?

Here's one a personal injury attorney client used.

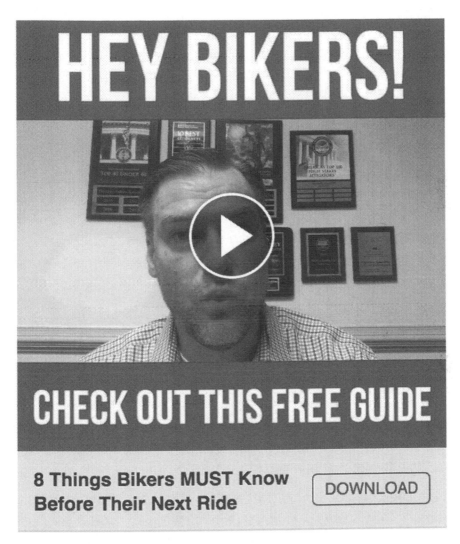

8 Things Bikers MUST Know Before Their Next Ride

[DOWNLOAD]

👍❤️😮 186   26 Comments   141 Shares

Every single day, he gets seven to ten new leads from that one video ad alone. Just be sure to avoid specific promises ("Make more money!") and the second person ("You...") so your ad doesn't get shut down.

The second essential element is **desire**. It's not enough to provide value. *Tell* people they're going to receive value—in no uncertain terms. If you know what your niche wants, it's very easy to give it to them. You interviewed at least ten people and created bait, so you're almost there. For me, I know lawyers want more law clients, more cases, and more income. That's why I call out their desire in the big red bar.

Hey lawyers, need law clients?

Call out your niche's desire in their own words.

Want more time with your kids?

Want creditors to stop calling you?

Want to protect your business from IP theft?

So, your niche stops scrolling and starts watching. Now, prove your **credibility** (the third essential element). Introduce yourself, tell a **story** about the **old method** (the fourth and fifth elements). Then explain why "the old way of doing things" doesn't work. Here's how my credibility intro starts:

> My name is Andrew Stickel, and I don't own a suit. But what I *do* do is I help more than fifty law firms get more clients from the most unlikely of sources, social media.

Okay, not *all* of my videos start this way. I recorded that particular ad in a t-shirt when I was at Dan Henry's house. I looked like I was there to do his plumbing. Didn't matter—the video converted anyway.

If you've appeared in major news publications or on TV, work those into your credibility intro. No one cares about you, so don't make your intro long. Prove your authority in one or two sentences, and get right to the story—the meat of your video. People relate to stories way more than facts and figures. In my t-shirt video, I talked about an estate planning law client who struggled with marketing.

I have a client named Aaron. He's an estate planning lawyer from Washington D.C. He's tried for a year to get leads from social media. He's failed time and time again. And the reason it's not working is because he's using the old method to get clients. I've got a new way that can help you.

Your story sets up the sixth essential element, an **opportunity switch**. The opportunity switch is the new opportunity that you're offering. This is where you let people know that *your* solution is superior to the "old way" of doing things. In my niche, lawyers like Aaron create post, after post, after post on social media. They *hope* somebody finds them, reads them, and books a consultation. That rarely happens. My new opportunity is creating *one* post with a valuable piece of content. It works much, much better than the hope-and-pray method.

What we do is we use one very specific type of ad. Instead of creating post, after post, after post, we create one specific post. This post not only brings in more leads, it brings in high quality leads which lead to more cases. And more cases lead to more revenue.

You can easily apply this element to your first (or next) video ad script. Be a little creative and think about how can you give your services a new twist. If you're a bankruptcy attorney, your old-versus-new opportunity story might sound like this:

The reason you're struggling is because you're paying the minimum payments on your credit cards every single month. A lot of people do that. But the problem is, by doing that, you're not actually paying down the balance. It's going to take you forty years, and you're never going to get your head above water. Paying the monthly minimum payments is a thing of the past.

The new way to deal with credit card debt is this. You can file for this thing called bankruptcy, and you'll consolidate all those payments into one monthly payment that you can afford. This way, you can stop the late payments.

Now, like I said, you want to tell a *story* to help illustrate your opportunity switch. Don't just say, "A lot of people do *this*, and the reason it doesn't work is because of *that*." Cut-and-dry, tell-it-like-it-is statements are not compelling, and your audience goes back to scrolling.

You need some sort of new opportunity pitted against an old method that just isn't working. Honestly, if the old method worked, why would your niche need you? That's the whole point here! Your story should illustrate why they need your services. For estate planning, the old method is leaving the fate of your family, your children, your house, your money, and your business up to the court. People assume estate planning is for old rich people. Then along comes you, an estate planning attorney, to introduce a new way:

What you can do is you can create this document, and I can help you do it. Should the worst happen, should you pass away, your wife doesn't have to worry. All she has to do is use this piece of paper. No questions. No worrying. No probate. In my upcoming webinar, I'll show you how to create your estate plan.

If you're a personal injury lawyer whose niche is motorcyclists, contrast old and new *technology*. You can say something like:

Wear this piece of gear to protect you from motorcycle accidents. Most people don't realize that you need this. They wear this old gear instead because that's been the common practice for so long, but technology's really advancing. We're finding that people who wear this one piece of gear see a twenty-seven percent reduction of head injuries.

Whatever problems the old method causes, they *cannot* be your audience's fault. People don't want to accept blame. That's why I don't tell attorneys the reason that social media isn't working is because they're not good at social media. I actually tried that once. The ad tanked. Nobody wants to hear they suck. I changed my tanking ad from, "You are not good at social media," to, "The method of social media marketing that you're using is a very common method. But it doesn't work. It's not your fault."

It's not your fault. Ah, what a magical sentence.

Years ago, some weight loss company advertised diet pills on late-night TV. One line stuck with me:

> You've struggled all this time, and you just can't lose weight. You've tried. You've dieted. You've exercised. You've done all that stuff, and it's not your fault.

Brilliant. They sold a crap load of diet pills because they let people off the hook. They basically said, "Look, the reason you couldn't lose weight was not because of you. It wasn't because you ate too much. It wasn't because you didn't exercise. It was because you were using the wrong system."

I'm sure the company got sued for selling a sketchy product. Nevertheless, still a great lesson for marketing a law firm. Tell your niche that the reason they're struggling is not any of their doing, it's because they used the wrong method. Externalize the blame, and your niche will love you. Marketing consultant Blair Warren put it this way:

> People will do anything for those who encourage their dreams, justify their failures, allay their fears, confirm their suspicions, and help them throw rocks at their enemies.[1]

Persuasion in one sentence. Even if your client is in jail, tell them it's not their fault. Take a criminal defense example. If you're a criminal defense lawyer targeting families of addicts, you can say:

> The problem is that addiction fuels crime. If someone has an addiction, they're not thinking clearly. They're only thinking about that addiction. They do whatever they have to do. They're breaking in and stealing, whatever it takes to get money to get one more hit. They get stuck in this vicious cycle where they break the law, go to jail, get out of jail, break the law again, and go back to jail. There is nothing to intervene. It's not their fault. The problem is that the system is broken.

> What we need to do is get your addicted loved one into a situation where, instead of going to jail, we intercept them. We help put them in a treatment program so they can get the help they need.

The key to a new opportunity that *is* a new opportunity is how you creatively package it. For example, let's say you're an estate planning attorney. You could create a "new product" for families to get their estates done. It's not necessarily a new opportunity, it's just *presented* as a new opportunity. Maybe you call the product "The Family Legacy Plan."

Are you a bankruptcy attorney? Maybe your product could be "The Stress Relief 2000." Just be careful that your new opportunity is not an *improvement*. Ask yourself, "Am I changing something, or am I improving what they're doing?"

For example, if I tell attorneys struggling with ads, "Hey, here's a way to make your ads better, grab my cheat sheet," I won't pick up many emails. My niche doesn't think social media ads work. So a "better" way to run ads won't sell.

If you're a bankruptcy attorney, your niche doesn't want "a better way to pay your monthly credit card bills." You need to come along and tell people about a completely different way to handle debt through consolidation. A new opportunity changes the game. It disrupts the status quo. So I might write my video script and say:

> Listen. The reason your social media ads don't work is because you're using an old method that doesn't work very well. But it's not your fault you weren't using the right method. I've got a new method. One that works extremely well. Let me tell you about the revolutionary new way to get law clients on social media.

As another example, I created a document for a family law attorney client called, "13 Reasons Children Benefit From Divorce." This bait pits the old way (staying together for the kids) against the new opportunity (getting divorced and being happy). If your cheat sheet (or free guide or webinar or training) is the bait, the opportunity switch is the hook, line, and sinker.

The seventh element is the **offer**. When I present my offer, I say, "If you would like to download a 100% no cost, step by step cheat sheet that shows you exactly how Aaron gets clients on social media, click this link..."

One crucial thing to notice about that last sentence—I rarely use the word "free" in social media ads. I say "no cost" instead. You can still use the word, but it's a good idea to not use it too often. Social media companies get really funny about financial claims, guarantees, and outcomes. If you want to talk about an outcome, talk about an outcome you *already* helped a client achieve, rather than promising an outcome to your viewers.

And now for the eighth and final element. Believe it or not, your video needs **instructions**. To just say, "Download my cheat sheet," and end the video is not enough. *Get specific.* Say, "Click on the link below. When you get to the link, you're going to see a button at the bottom. Click the button, enter your email address, and check your inbox." Remember, people are lazy. Make it really, really easy for them to take your bait. As soon as I added specific instructions to my video ads, I saw opt-ins skyrocket.

You can even *show* your niche what to expect. Use screencast software (like Screencast-O-Matic) to show someone filling out the form on your landing page. That way, when they click and see your landing page, there are no surprises—it's not the first time they've been there. Believe it or not, this *does* improve conversions.

Implement these eight elements when filming your video ad, and you'll have killer bait that's (almost) ready to throw into the water.

If You're Boring, You're Broke

Now you know what you need to create an amazing script as your foundation for a high converting video ad. But the script is just *what* you say, not *how* you say it. The seventh element is your on-camera performance, and it makes or breaks your advertisement. Don't break into a cold sweat just yet. Let's face it—most lawyers aren't exciting. Not to single you out personally. We've all seen the hokey local TV ads of a blank-faced lawyer staring into the camera competing for Most Boring Ad Of The Year.

Just as they say the camera adds ten pounds, the camera sucks away any and all energy that you have. So if you speak normally, you're going to seem really, really, *really* bland. If you look dead and have zero energy on-camera, that's going to come across. Passion for anything is infectious. People pick up on how passionate you are about a subject. Excitement boosts your credibility.

Think about actors. There are so many different ways somebody can interpret a script. When auditions are held for a part, fifty people go for the same role, and they all read the same lines. Only one person gets the role—the person who most enthusiastically embraces the character. In your video ads, play a more exciting version of yourself. Vary your inflection. Avoid monotone. Go over the top.

Most people can't memorize a script and record the entire thing in one take. That's fine. I recommend "quick cut videos." It's easy—all you do is record one line at a time. You say it over, and over, and over again until you get it right. Then you go onto the next line, and you say that line over, and over, and over. You can say it wrong twenty times. If you get it right on the twenty-first, perfect. You only need one.

If you hire a freelance video editor, they're going to remove those twenty low-energy versions. All you have left are short clips, which your editor compiles. They cut right before you start the sentence and cut right after you finish. No pauses, no delays. You want people watching to not be able to get a single thought in. Bam, bam, bam. That quick, that tight. Give viewers half a second to think about something else, and you've lost them.

Read this sentence.

NOWREADTHISSENTENCE.

See what I mean? No spaces, no pauses, no time to let your mind wander. Extremely quick cuts often don't even *look* edited. It's not until after people see your videos two or three times that they notice your video isn't all one take. Do they care? Nope. Not if you're providing high value.

Put a cherry on top with music. Tell your freelance video editor to add a background track. Music changes the feel of a video, adding drive and energy. I usually go with energetic rock music and pick a popular track on an inexpensive stock music website like AudioJungle.net for under $20.

Give Your Niche What They Want (To Read)

The last thing you put in your ad is the ad itself—the ad copy, specifically, which appears *above* your video ad on social media. You have two options. Talk about the benefits, or talk about the new opportunity. In one of my cheat sheet ads, I describe the new opportunity:

> Most lawyers struggle to get leads using social media because they use a very old but very common method that almost everyone uses. What if I told you there was a new method that allows you to get way better leads at a much better cost, and not many people know about it? If you'd like to learn all about this method, download our no-cost cheat sheet here.

My personal injury attorney client uses the benefits option in his cheat sheet ad copy:

This no-cost cheat sheet reveals:

- A factor found in 26% of all motorcycle deaths in 2016

- Two things all motorcycle helmets must have

- Which gear helps protect bikers from the most common injuries

- An assumption bikers should never make while riding— doing so can be deadly

I've been finding more and more that curiosity alone works extremely well.

This factor was found in 26% of all motorcycle fatalities in 2016. Download this cheat sheet to learn what it is.

Depending on which ad platform you use, you get multiple options for your call-to-action button. On Facebook, you can choose action verbs like "Download," "Learn More," or "Get Offer."

Facebook also offers a space for your ad headline, which appears *below* your video. I repurpose the title of my bait for the headline. If yours is longer, trim a few words off.

The three secrets to getting more law clients from social media.

Eight things bikers must know before their next ride.

Since you've done your homework with your Ask Campaign, you know what your niche wants and what they don't want. So, write a headline that grabs their attention as they scroll down their social media feeds. If you're struggling to come up with a great attention-grabbing headline, try using your how-to-without statement.

Thousands of Leads for Hundreds of Pennies

Ads aren't free. Unfortunately. But social media advertising is the next best thing. My rule of thumb is to spend $20 to $30 per day on ads, or $600 to $900 per month. Unlike Google PPC ads, you're paying for *reach*, not *clicks*. So if you spend $30 per day, you reach more people than you do with $20.

If you want to see which niche segment responds best to your ads, split test different demographics. (Currently, Facebook allows you to do this.) If you spend $30 a day, divide that between the sexes—$15 a day to women and $15 a day to men. You can also split your ad campaign by age. Cut what doesn't work, do more of what does. Easy, right?

Put $10 a day for ages twenty-four to forty, $10 for ages forty-one to fifty, and $10 for fifty-one to sixty-five, and so on. Whatever you test, test it for a week and then take a peek at the results. Facebook is pretty amazing. Their ad platform shows you exactly who engages, shares, and clicks your ads more. You can even see who makes it to your landing page and subscribes!

Of course, if you *want* to spend more on ads, do it. It's all about reach. If I'm testing multiple audiences at once, I'll spend anywhere from $50 to $200 a day on ads. When I find what works, I scale up until it stops working.

One of my personal injury attorneys averages ten new biker leads every day on way less than that. Just imagine. In a year of working with me and running these ads, he'll have 3,600 people in his online community and on his email list (owned traffic). Think about that. 3,600 people who all ride motorcycles *and* look up to this attorney as the go-to motorcycle accident guy. In fact, members now create more content in his group than he does.

The question is, how does he *keep* these members in his group? What stops them from hitting that dreaded "unsubscribe" button? What does he do to create a sense of community and motivate people to create original content? And how does he turn as many leads into clients as soon as possible when they join?

These are all questions that I'm going to answer. In the next chapter.

Chapter 5
Your Law Firm's Greatest Asset

Shark Tank For Lawyers?

Most people who watch *Shark Tank* miss one of the most powerful marketing secrets on the planet. Maybe you spotted it. It's rare for a budding entrepreneur to see their startup capital dreams come true.[1] When someone *does* reach a deal with one of the Sharks, it has less to do with charm and way more to do with the right *channel*.

For example, have you ever noticed how inventor Lori Greiner almost never takes a deal that doesn't work on QVC, the Home Shopping Network, or Bed, Bath, & Beyond? Almost every deal FUBU founder Daymond John takes distributes products through retail outlets. And Mr. Wonderful himself—Kevin O'Leary—brags about his connections to wholesaler Costco.

Each of the Sharks has their own distribution channel. An existing, successful pipeline to launch products to customers who already exist. Forget the billions of dollars and the flashy personalities for a minute. The Sharks' most valuable asset is a distribution channel that they already have in place.

A lot of lawyers have distribution channels, but very few own them. For example, a billboard could be a distribution channel. The problem, however, is the billboard costs you money, and it isn't controllable. You can't control who sees it, and you can't retarget anyone who did. The same goes for TV advertisements. Sure, they're a channel (literally), but if someone cancels their cable bill next month, you have no way to put your law firm in front of them again.

The distribution channel *you're* going to create is very different. Because you control everything, it'll be your law firm's most valuable asset. The best part? It will only take you *minutes per day* to manage.

Lead Your Niche—They're Begging You

Time for a quick recap. You have a niche. You know what they want. And you gave it to them (via your ad, bait, and landing page). Next up, your distribution channel—a social media group you turn into a highly engaged, insanely profitable community.

In the past, people congregated online in private forums and on message boards. Recently, Facebook groups have become the hot place to gather. (The community building strategy explored in this chapter works with any social media group platform, such as LinkedIn Groups.)

Once your niche takes your bait and opts into your email list, you have their contact information. Good for you! You've now converted them into traffic you own. So, you can follow up with them over, and over, and over again, continuing to provide value. (More on daily outreach in Chapter 6.)

You can even reach out to people personally right after they download your bait. Ask if they have questions related to the cheat sheet they received. A decent percentage of people will respond. They'll have a question that leads to a consultation, which leads to a new client for you.

No, you're not violating solicitation laws by doing this. You don't have to ask anyone's permission to talk about the law and educate people. You're not offering unsolicited legal advice. You're providing value. Angela Langlock, a trademark and business law attorney, put it this way:

I've been using social media to build my law practice. I think one of the perceived reasons why lawyers aren't doing social media marketing is because they are afraid of the Bar. "Oh, is it advertising? Do I have to comply with the advertising rules?" Actually, if you look at most of the advertising rules, social media isn't considered attorney advertising. I have the right to get on and talk about the law. I don't have to ask anybody's permission to talk about the law.

If the people you're educating aren't ready to hire you right now, that's fine. They opted in. So, every person is interested in *something* related to the services that you provide. Very good news. Now, it's time to push them into your social media group. As I mentioned before, all you need to do is link to your group in your email with the bait they requested. I also tell people to join my group in Youtube video descriptions, on my LinkedIn profile, on my Instagram profile, and in the footer of every email.

Once people join your group, they'll start looking at you as the authority in your field.

The secret is, you're not *asking* them, "Would you like to join my group?" You're *telling* them to join. Like Jay Abraham says:

People are silently begging to be led.[2]

Most people who download your bait will, in fact, join your group if you tell them to.

So create one.

When you're building your community, think about the *benefits* you can offer. What are the wants and needs of your niche? What legal issues do they see as a struggle? When you're coming up with a name for your group, these questions matter—a LOT.

If you're an employment law attorney, for example, don't build a group called Employment Law Facebook Group. Is your niche Walmart employees? Then name your group Employees of Walmart. If your niche is female professionals targeted by sexual harassers, start a group called Stop Workplace Harassment.

As you know, my Facebook group is Lawyer Marketing. I didn't name it Andrew Stickel's Facebook Group because nobody knows who that is. They don't care about me (or you). Everyone's favorite topic is themselves. It's basic psychology. People only do things (like join a social media group) if they expect to *get* something out of it. If a lawyer sees Lawyer Marketing, and they own their own law firm, they're probably going to be interested. In fact, *most* lawyers have to handle their own marketing. Why no law school courses touch on marketing is beyond me.

Now, your niche doesn't have to be flashy to make the most of your social media group. Community building works for injury lawyers, criminal defense lawyers, family lawyers, business lawyers, immigration lawyers, real estate lawyers, bankruptcy lawyers, estate planning lawyers, mass tort lawyers, social security lawyers, workers comp lawyers, tax lawyers, product liability lawyers, and more.

Quick research reveals several examples of niche communities that lawyers could build. For example, the Facebook group Traumatic Brain Injury Healing and Recovery Support Group has 7,500 members. Personal injury lawyers, take note!

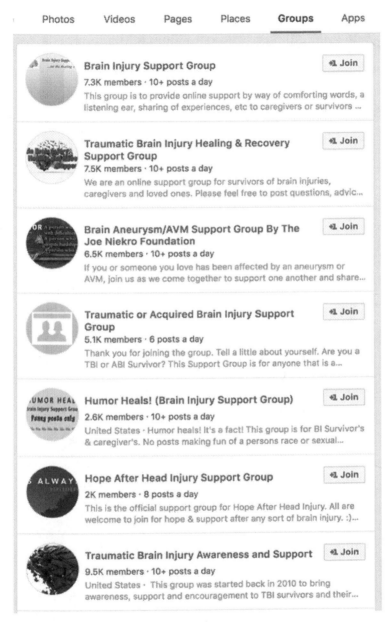

There are also groups that help family members of those dealing with addiction. Affected by Addiction Support Group has over *66,000* members. This would be a great place for a criminal defense lawyer to start posting and providing value.

Affected By Addiction Support Group

+1 Join

66K members · 10+ posts a day

United States · The mission of Affected By Addiction is to ensure a safe space and reduce the stigma for the nearly 1 in 2 American...

Addiction Recovery Support Group

+1 Join

11K members · 10+ posts a day

This is a judgement free group for people in recovery and people seeking recovery and/or attempting to get and stay clean. This isn't ...

Drug/Alcohol Addiction Support Group

+1 Join

6.9K members · 10+ posts a day

BE AWARE THAT THIS GROUP IS NOT FOR PUSHERS ATTEMPTING TO SELL / SUPPLY DRUGS TO MEMBERS IN RECOVERY, NOR WILL...

If your niche is Second Amendment advocates and gun enthusiasts, you're in luck. A page called U.S. LawShield has amassed a following of over 118,000 people. This isn't a Facebook *group*, it's a *page*. If I owned or managed the page, I would push as many of these people as possible into a group to build a community.

If you're a family law attorney, you could build a community inspired by groups that already exist. Take Separated and Divorce Support Group with its 45,000-plus members.

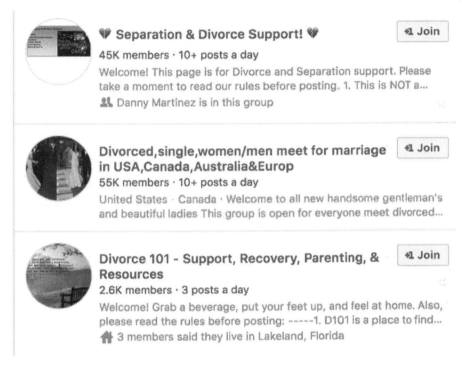

Bankruptcy attorney? Help people target debt. Groups like Debt to Success System, Free Credit Repair and Debt Settlement Information, and Ditch Your Debt boast thousands of members each.

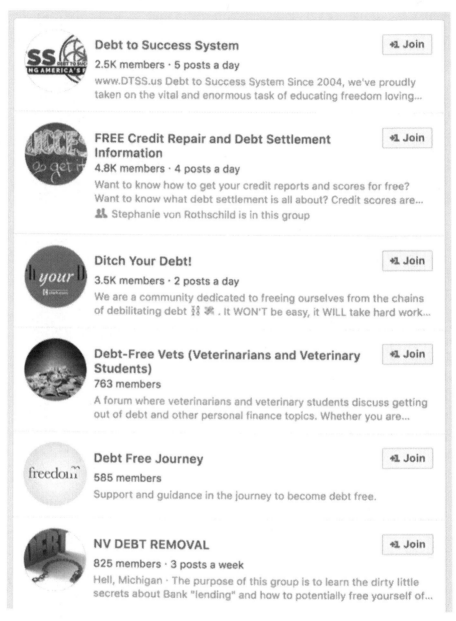

Immigration lawyer? You guessed it—your niche already has groups, too. Russians in Los Angeles has 9,000 members, and Indians in Atlanta has over 21,000!

Russians in Los Angeles

+1 Join

9K members · 10+ posts a day

Los Angeles, California · This group is intended for all Russian speakers in Los Angeles, regardless of where they were born....

Indians in Atlanta

+1 Join

21K members · 10+ posts a day

Johns Creek, Georgia · An ounce of help is better than a pound of preaching. Admin is not responsible for any dispute in Sales or...

Employment Lawyer? Do you think you might be able to get employment cases out of groups like Ex-Employees of GT or FedEx Employees?

EX Employees of GTE

+1 Join

9.7K members · 7 posts a day

For all Ex employees (co-workers) to refind each other and remember GTE before it was Verizon

🏠 40 members said they live in Lakeland, Florida

USPS Non-Career Employees

+1 Join

1.4K members · 4 posts a day

United States · Do you feel that management is taking advantage of you? Do you feel your union could intervene more? Do you want to...

Amtrak Employees

+1 Join

6.6K members · 10+ posts a day

This is a closed group of present, past or retired Amtrak Employees, and Henry. This is not a "Rail Buff" site. Amtrak Family only please.

FedEx Employees

+1 Join

12K members · 10+ posts a day

Hello, and welcome to the FedEx family! This is a closed, private group that exists for ALL employees of FedEx, past and present...

I could keep going, but you get the idea. What's crazy about these groups is *hardly any of them are owned by lawyers*. Imagine the terrible advice that people are giving and receiving in those groups. They're not lawyers, they're everyday Joes and Janes who Google their problems. *You* are the legal authority in your niche, and it's incredibly easy to position yourself as such. Remember, ninety-five percent of success is just showing up.

These groups are all examples. Don't go invading existing Facebook groups with spammy posts. Renee may have succeeded when she co-opted other people's social media groups, but she did it very, very carefully. She never pitched her services, she only provided lots of value.

I recommend you start your own group. That way, *you* control the traffic. You control nothing in someone else's group. Every new member in *your* group is either a prospective client or someone who can refer prospective clients.

Remember my personal injury attorney client's motorcycle rider group? In four months, he had nearly eight *hundred* members and is continuing to add new members at a rate of ten per day. People now create more than half of all content on their own. It's taking off as its own living, breathing community, and members feel involved. One member recently got into an accident, pulled out their camera, took video of the damage, and posted it in the group.

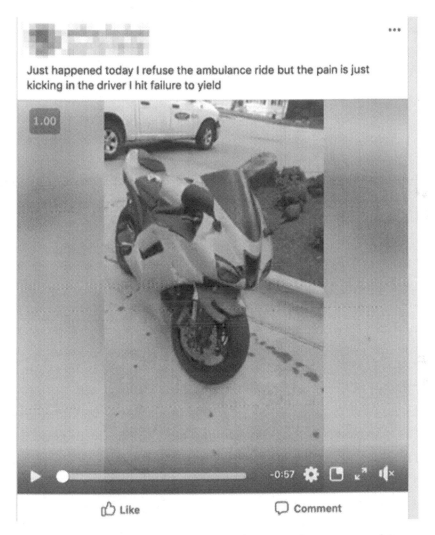

Just happened today I refuse the ambulance ride but the pain is just kicking in the driver I hit failure to yield

He contacted the person as soon as he saw the post, and it was a great case. Oh, and did I mention this happened only *eleven days* after my client started his Facebook group?

If you want to see the exact step by step strategy we used, visit

www.getlawfirmclients.com/training

for a walkthrough.

I caught up with my client and asked about his growing biker community.

"It's crazy, Andy," he said. "Every day, I'm attracting more and more potential clients using this strategy. My group is giving me an unfair advantage over all the other personal injury attorneys in my area."

That means a *lot*. Because he's in one of the top ten most saturated law firm markets—Atlanta. He got a wrongful death case within *eight* weeks. It blows my mind how few attorneys outside of my clients create and leverage social media groups. Can you think of any other attorneys in your market doing this? Probably not, and that's good for you! There's no competition. Forget battling with every other attorney in your market over the top spot on Google. No need to outbid them on Google AdWords. Community building is where it's at. (More on actually closing clients inside of your group in Chapter 7.)

How did that Atlanta attorney get his first lead from his group in less than two weeks? And how can *you*? The fact is, people won't just post a video of their wrecked bike (or marriage license, or tax return, or whatever) in your group unless they want your help. So, nurture that trust and engage *every* community member one-on-one.

If you wait until *after* they join, you're too late. Confused? Social media platforms like Facebook let you engage people *before* they join your group. You can require that people *ask* to join. All you need are a few easy questions. I like to repurpose questions from my Ask Campaign.

What's the number one thing you'd like to learn regarding _____?

You also need to ask a question that will come in handy when people invite their friends and family to join.

What is your email address?

This question might seem redundant. After all, your video ad sends people to your group, and you already have *their* emails. But the fact is, people might join your group organically, not from the bait via email. And what if Mark Zuckerberg decides he doesn't like Facebook groups anymore? Or maybe just *your* group gets shut down. Or maybe Facebook has a scandal worse than the Cambridge Analytica fiasco, and *they* get shut down.

Although it's unlikely, the group you worked so hard to build *could* go away just like that, and all those members with it. No warnings. You have no way to contact the hundreds or thousands of people who joined the group organically (not through your video ad and email list). If you didn't get *those* members' email addresses, that's it. They're gone. You can hope and pray that they'll find you again. But I wouldn't take that chance.

Internet marketer Jonny West tried to log onto Facebook one day, but he couldn't. Facebook deleted his personal profile, his business page, his growing group, everything. He never got an explanation. If he hadn't made a point to collect his followers' and leads' emails, his million-dollar business would now be closed.

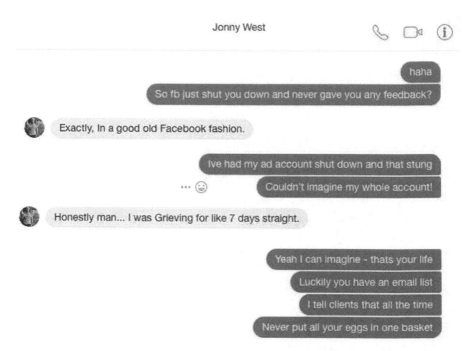

Jonny West

haha

So fb just shut you down and never gave you any feedback?

Exactly, In a good old Facebook fashion.

Ive had my ad account shut down and that stung

... 😔

Couldn't imagine my whole account!

Honestly man... I was Grieving for like 7 days straight.

Yeah I can imagine - thats your life

Luckily you have an email list

I tell clients that all the time

Never put all your eggs in one basket

I'm not trying to scare you. Frankly, I don't see Facebook going away anytime soon. Zuck himself believes in the groups feature. He told users in a 2018 announcement to "expect more" from Facebook groups because many have become "tight-knit communities."[3]

Even if groups stand the test of internet time, your organic reach may drop off. Years ago, Facebook business page owners could reach 20% of their followers with every post. For free! Pretty decent if you had a big number of followers. If 10,000 people liked your page, Facebook showed your every post to 2,000 of them. That's enough to build your business!

Today, countless anecdotes suggest that Facebook shows fewer than 0.5% of business page posts to followers. It's not even worth it. You can't run a business using a free Facebook page anymore. What if Facebook groups go the same way? Right now, I get 35% to 75% reach, but what if it drops down to 0.5%? My group isn't useless, but it's no longer a powerful distribution channel. More like a distribution trickle.

Regardless of what happens, you *must* ask people for their email address when they join your group. It's good business. Yes, groups are the number-one (yet little-known) distribution channel for law firms today. Yes, you control ad traffic and group membership. But only people who subscribe to your email list constitute *traffic you own*. When people request to join Lawyer Marketing, what do you think is the first question they see?

Lawyer Marketing

Closed Group · 803 Members   ✕

Please answer these questions from the admins. It helps them review membership requests and only they can see your answers.

Questions · 3

Want my no-cost cheat sheet "The 3 Secrets to Getting More Law Clients on Social Media?" If so, please enter your email address.   •••

Write an answer...

What law firm marketing topics would you like to learn about?   •••

Write an answer...

[REQUIRED] What Is the Name of Your Law Firm? What Area of Law Do You Practice? (Sorry, this group is for lawyers only.)   •••

Send to Admins

Traffic I control becomes traffic I own. It's possible that new members found my group because they for asked my cheat sheet and read my email. If so, they'll either type their email again or ignore it. In either case, I lose nothing. As of this writing, I have *four times* as many email addresses as Lawyer Marketing members. People delete Facebook, but they don't ever delete their emails.

Now, if you just say, "Please give me your email address," nobody will. So package your request in value—dangle your bait again. That's how I always get lawyers' email addresses. Sometimes twice. I don't care because I don't have to. I use inexpensive software (Group Funnels and Zapier) to integrate new members' answers with my email list. Any duplicates are automatically ignored.

Otherwise, the only way you can capture new members' email addresses is if you write them down or copy-and-paste manually. If you've got ten, fifty, or a hundred people joining every day, that's a full-time job you don't want. My rule of thumb is, if I *can* automate a task, I *should*.

Another option is to hire a Virtual Assistant, which I also do. If you want to see how I hire world-class talent for a few dollars per hour, visit www.getlawfirmclients.com/training for tips.

Whatever you do, *do not* skip the email collection step. If your group goes the way of the dinosaur for any reason, you're screwed—if you don't have members' email addresses. Your social media group is a marketing *tool*, not the marketing *strategy*. The most important marketing strategy is to build your email list (traffic you own). Take care of that, and you can have a field day in your group without looking back over your shoulder.

Getting Engaged

So, people in your niche join your niche group. And they tell you what they want when they join (because you asked). Great! Now, how do you *keep* them in your group?

It's all about engagement. The first thing you want new members to see is a post welcoming them. As with your advertising, choose video over plain text. Record a two to three minute video. Tell new members why you started the group and what value you are going to provide. Borrow your credibility intro from your video ad. Give the links to your website and your other social media profiles to close out the video.

When you publish the video, include text above it in the post itself. The text should say, "Welcome to _____! Thanks for joining us!" Then ask questions that get people talking about themselves. I ask new members in Lawyer Marketing, "What type of law do you practice? How long have you been a lawyer? Where do you practice?" I've got dozens of comments on that one welcome post, all new members happy to introduce themselves.

I also recommend you engage new members inside your group. Every week, Facebook prompts me to write a post welcoming new members. When I take Facebook up on the offer, the post *automatically* tags all the new people. All I have to do is write a quick welcome, publish the post, and Facebook instantly notifies all new members. How cool is that?

When you first start your group, you'll recognize most new members as people who took your bait. Over time, you want to grow your group *outside* of your own network—without advertising. I'm talking about *organic* growth. Your group grows without you paying for it. The good news is, Facebook helps you do this. Did you know that Facebook suggests new groups to users based on their interests? Well, they do, and you can take advantage of it!

The way to show up in these suggested groups is engagement. The more often your posts get lots of likes and comments, the more Facebook showcases your group. I bet Zuck is over there thinking, *Okay, if there's a lot of action in here, this group must be growing and doing well. I'm going to show the group to more people.*

After people join, encourage engagement with questions. I do this in Lawyer Marketing all the time. Remember this post?

 **Andy Stickel** •••
🛡 **Admin** · March 17

I've been getting a ton of messages on Facebook from some members of this group asking how to get more clients from social media.

I already put out a free cheat sheet, but I'm thinking of doing a free live video training covering this subject.

Would anyone be interested in this?

I've gotten hundreds of comments on posts like this. Every time I post a question that gets great engagement, I see an influx of new members. All that engagement sends Lawyer Marketing back to the suggested groups section.

If you're running out of ideas for new bait, ask people what they want to learn about. Ask, "What topics do you want me to cover in my upcoming video?" and you'll get a *lot* of engagement.

I also recommend spying on other groups. If you're a family law attorney building a parenting group, check out other parenting groups. See what the hot topics are, and bring them back to yours as questions. Ask, "What's your morning routine?" or, "How often do you exercise?" Simple questions get lots of answers. Not everything you post has to be about your law firm. In fact, it's better if your content varies.

Back when the World Cup was underway, I put up a post asking members which country they thought would win. Hundreds of back-and-forth comments brought even more lawyers into the group. All from an unrelated post about sports!

Get people talking, and Facebook gets to suggesting. You're a real person, after all. You've got real people in your group, so make it a community. If you're at a business function, you don't *only* talk business. You ask people about their hobbies and interests to discover what you have in common. Your social media group is no different. *It's online networking*. You're asking questions, having conversations, and building rapport—and that invaluable *trust*.

I have some lawyer clients who test controversy. Controversial topics get better engagement. Obviously. But use controversy at your own risk. Me? I avoid it. I don't want to risk alienating half of my potential clients. In today's polarized environment, I avoid all politics and all religion.

Maybe you disagree. If you're a criminal defense attorney targeting Second Amendment advocates, talk guns. Be my guest. Give members the chance to voice their conservative opinions, and they'll relate to you better. As long as you agree with them! You still run the risk of turning *some* people off. If you don't want to take a side, you could ask an open-ended question like, "What do you think of this new gun control bill?" If you do take a side, you'll lose some people. But you'll get better engagement from the people who stick with you because they'll trust you more. You're one of them.

Whether you avoid incendiary topics or throw fuel on the fire, always, always, *always* use a picture. Even if the picture has nothing to do with what you're talking about. For example, in my post about my free live video training idea, my picture was simply the word, "ATTENTION!"

Why? Because I want my post to do exactly that. Get attention. Whenever I post text in my group without a picture, nobody engages. Even if I ask a great question. When your group members are scrolling through their newsfeed, pictures catch their eye. Finding the right picture is as easy as a Google Images search for words like, "Hey," "Hello," "Attention," "Questions," "Help," or "Opinions?" Pick a photo with bright colors, and you'll get even better results.

Help Mark Zuckerberg Help You

Automated pre-tagging and suggested groups are two ways Facebook helps community builders. But that's not all. Zuck also wants to help you post regular content. It's good for him, and it's great for you! So, take advantage of Facebook's post scheduling feature.

I schedule my group posts two weeks out, two videos per day, five days a week. The data reveals the best time to post and get engagement is between 1:00 and 3:00 PM local time.[4] Engagement drops like crazy on Saturdays and Sundays, so I don't waste my content on the weekends.

Think about the average person during the average workday. Before noon, they're hungry and distracted. After lunch comes the afternoon lull. They feel a little drowsy. They find a few minutes to play around on social media. And that's when your group posts show up in their newsfeed.

After thirty or forty videos, you can start recycling your content. (More on how to create these videos in Chapter 6.) If you're adding new members every single day (and you will), your old videos are *new* to them. No one who joined Lawyer Marketing today saw the videos I posted last week, last month, or two months ago.

Plus, no video ever gets 100% viewership. Anywhere from three out of ten to seven out of ten people see content you post in the group. I've got so much content, and I don't want it to go to waste. You will, too. But don't start your recycling until you hit the thirty to forty video mark. You don't want to keep posting the same videos too soon. The videos should not be extremely familiar (or easily forgettable). Reuse your content as many times as you want, just not until you've hit your minimum number of videos. You still want your group members seeing fresh, high-value content every single day. That's how you make your group invaluable. I've learned that even if people don't leave a comment, they *do* watch my videos. Facebook's video viewership metrics tell that story. They'll tell yours, too.

Value, Yes. Perfection, No.

Like running your Ask Campaign or writing your clickbait title, community building has a learning curve. And that's perfectly fine. When I started Lawyer Marketing, I *sucked*. For about a month and a half, the only members were me, my business partner, a few friends, and my mom (seriously). But climbing the learning curve made a huge difference for me. I learned how to talk on camera, create high-value content, and post questions people wanted to answer. By the time I felt comfortable managing my group, my content was *so* valuable that lawyers asked about hiring me *hours* after they joined.

As long as you're providing value to your niche group, you don't have to get everything perfect. They don't care. They need your help. Provide value, become the authority, get clients. In that order.

I might sound like a broken record, but I can't emphasize value enough. So many small business owners create communities, and all they do is sell their stuff. Over, and over, and over again. I've been able to thrive in an environment where lawyers get hit up by marketing companies left and right. A lot of them got burned by marketing companies. So, when I provide value, I'm the one and only marketing authority they trust. And as you know, authority is power. Because *I'm* the authority in law firm marketing, why would a lawyer hire anybody else? The same applies to your law firm.

If you're an expert on construction accidents, for example, put out helpful content. Talk about how construction workers can stay safe and what people should do when accidents do happen. When somebody in your construction workers community gets into an accident, why would they call anybody else? You're *the* expert on construction accidents. You can apply this to any field and any practice area for law.

And to sweeten the pot, when you become the authority, people actually try to convince *you* to work with *them*! If you can provide value for someone, they're going to trust you. And eventually, when they *do* want to hire you (and they will) they're going to reach out and beg you to help them. So, how do you make that inevitable?

Chapter 6
The Daily Value System

Don't Think (Or Work) Twice

So, you have all this traffic you own. Your community grows. And they trust you. This is an amazing start. But traffic, groups, and trust mean nothing *if* they don't result in more cases for your law firm. Not everyone is ready to hire you right now, and that's okay. Not all of the bikers in my attorney client's Georgia rider group crashed yesterday (thank God). But when catastrophe strikes, you want them thinking, *I have to talk to [your name] ASAP!*

Just because you're an authority doesn't mean you have top of mind awareness. They're two separate things. Now that people *know* you're the authority, they need to *remember* you at the right time. Like when a driver t-bones their bike, their spouse files for divorce, or when a business partner screws them over. And the most effective, most cost-efficient way to create that precious top of mind awareness is daily value.

Well, of course it is, you're thinking. *That's what you've been saying all along.*

You're right. But *knowing* that you should provide consistent value to your community isn't enough. You're busy. You have clients. Appointments. Responsibilities. And on top of all that, a family. Time is short. That's why I propose implementing a *system* as the best way to easily (and quickly) create daily value. And this chapter is all about that system.

With a good system, you don't have to think twice. You don't have to wrack your brain every time you sit down to write an email. And you don't have to somehow find time to write a thousand words a day on your law firm blog. That's how you burn out fast and hard. It's also how you get stuck in feast-or-famine content creation cycles. Your community hears from you for a few weeks, then nothing for a month. Then inspiration strikes you out of nowhere, and you crank out a week's worth of emails and schedule a dozen Facebook group posts. But then your distribution channel pumps a huge case into your firm, and you disappear to all but your new client for six months.

I see a better way. Systems—set 'em and forget 'em. The best part about my daily value system is that you only have to create *one* piece of content. Not a video, plus a blog article, plus an email, plus a social media post. Just *one video*. But you turn that one video into everything else—an article, and an email, and a social media post. That's the power of syndication.

Trademark and business law attorney Angela Langlock tested content creation and syndication for a week—and just that fast, she got clients. All she does is record one short, live Facebook video every week day and talk about trademark law. She answers frequently asked questions about Intellectual Property, for example. She closes each video with a free strategy session offer. It's really a consultation, but "free strategy session" doesn't sound nearly as intimidating to her business owner prospects.

After Angela records each live video, she syndicates. She transcribes the video, and publishes the text *and* the video on her blog as an article. That article gets pushed out to her social media profiles, such as LinkedIn, Instagram, and Twitter. Then she takes that same video-turned-article and emails it to her list, who already likes and trusts her.

To Angela's following, she looks like a content creation machine. But all it takes is a few minutes each morning. Hundreds of people watch and share her videos and articles every single day.

The secret, of course, is she provides value. *Consistently.* No matter what you do, if you provide value, you cannot go wrong. Provide value consistently, and now you've achieved that top of mind awareness your competition spends millions of dollars to get.

As an attorney, you have the opportunity to get in on the ground floor. So few lawyers use social media effectively, much less video or content syndication. Initially, the idea of appearing on camera five days a week freaked Angela out. But she thought, *You know what? If I'm doing video, and if I'm engaging, and if I know what I'm talking about, what better way is there to communicate with potential clients?* I sure can't think of one.

No More Writer's Block

Like Angela, I don't have time to write, edit, and proof blog articles every day, much less a few times a week. And neither do you. That's why video is the linchpin of my high-value content syndication system. Without a quick, easy way to produce content, *we just won't do it*.

Writing a blog post takes me hours, sometimes days because I obsess about it over, and over, and over again. But *anyone* can take five minutes and shoot a video. Even on my thirteen-hour work days, I can make time for several.

Another upside to video? It allows you to grow a large content library *very* quickly. Go to my YouTube channel, and you'll see literally hundreds of lawyer marketing videos. Even *I'm* shocked. It feels like I haven't put much effort into it.

If you spend five minutes every week day on video, it adds up. After three months you've got fifty to sixty videos. That's why a system is so important. You repeat the process over and over without thinking about it. Each video is another hook in the water you're going to use to catch your clients. You never know what topic will resonate the most with people. I've syndicated videos before thinking, *Oh man, this is a great video. Lawyers are going to love this!* But the thing flops. Then I'll throw something up one day when I'm really rushed, and *that's* the one that gets a ton of engagement—comments, questions, even inquiries. You never know what will click with people, so create it all.

Every piece of content gives you massive reach. I can take one video and reach potentially millions of people through my blog, on LinkedIn, Instagram, and Twitter. That's not even including traffic I control and own—my Lawyer Marketing Facebook group and growing email list!

But before you press the record button, let's think about your future content library at a high level. Over time, you're going to build this massive catalog of content in your group, on your blog, and all over social media. And people are going to binge-watch it. And the more of your high-value content prospects consume, the more likely they'll become leads—and clients.

People will perceive you as a trusted authority, a credible expert, and a leader. When you look at the leader of every movement throughout history, that leader is always an attractive character. I'm not talking looks, I'm talking *traits*. In your own way, you're leading a movement. You're the esteemed legal authority in your niche. And you're providing value unlike anything your competition offers. You, my friend, are an attractive character in the making.

Legal Attraction

Russell Brunson, author of *Dotcom Secrets* and *Expert Secrets*, taught me about attractive characters. Whether they're history's greatest heroes or attorneys like you, attractive characters have several traits in common. Once you understand these traits, you'll understand how to craft them into your videos—and build up a massive following.

The first trait all attractive characters have is a backstory. What drives you to practice law? How can your niche relate to you? And it can't be about the money. If you're a personal injury attorney, your backstory could revolve around a client early in your career who changed everything for you.

What inspires me about marketing for attorneys is pretty simple—I like helping people. I see how lawyers get screwed over and over again by marketing companies, and I decided that I wanted to give back. There's a lot of bad information out there, and I've had to go through all of it on my journey to learn how to market law firms. I tell this story, and anyone who's got a law firm and needs to market it can relate.

Attractive characters usually speak in parables. People relate to stories more than facts and figures. If you're a family law attorney who helps unhappy couples navigate divorce and child custody, record a video about the hazards of social media. Now, you *could* say, "Listen, you should never post about social activities on social media. Your spouse can go on there and take screenshots of you bragging about going out, partying, and acting irresponsibly. They can use that against you in court."

But that's all facts, no feelings. An attractive character tells a story instead, "I want to tell you a story about why you shouldn't post about social activities on social media. I had a client not long ago. Before she hired my firm, she decided to go out one night to party with her friends. It just so happened that it was her week to have custody of the kids. Her friends tagged her in photos and at bars on Facebook. Her ex-husband saw all those tags. He knew it was her night to have the kids. He downloaded all those pictures, saved the time stamps, and presented them in court. Now she has to pay child support!"

If you're married with children and you're going through a divorce, you can't get ahold of this attorney fast enough. Of course, if you talk about a client, don't share their personal information. But the scenario doesn't have to be *your* client—maybe it's just a story you heard. You're not under oath. If you're trying to make a point, just make the point.

Now for my best video recording tip—screw up. A lot. I'm kidding. Well, *half*-kidding. Even attractive characters have character flaws. People cannot relate to perfect people. This makes your life a *lot* easier, because you won't have to worry about getting every video perfect. The other day, my dog barked in the background while I was recording, and my wife called out to the dog. I could've redone the video. I didn't feel like it. After I posted it, I got engagement on the video because people were asking what kind of dog I had, and talking about their dogs. No one cared that the video wasn't perfect. In fact, the video did better *because* it wasn't perfect. Don't worry about recording perfect videos. Just worry about getting them done. Done is better than perfect.

Every published video gives you a leg up on your competition. How many attorneys targeting your same niche create videos? Not many. If any! So it doesn't matter if the lighting isn't perfect, or your phone goes off mid-recording. In many cases, perceived perfection hurts you. So, show your vulnerability. Show that you're flawed. When I caught up with Angela and asked about her experience with video, she made this exact point.

"Attorneys are worried that they're going to be perceived as less professional," she said. "I've got a secret for you—the less professional we seem, the more people can relate to us. We lawyers are really intimidating to people! We have all this knowledge. It's like we're God. But we're just people, too."

Besides making mistakes (and being okay with them), attractive characters create polarity. They don't want *everyone* to like them— only the *right* people. If you're a personal injury attorney targeting the biker niche, get on their side. Say, "Look, a lot of motorists out there aren't paying attention. They're careless and reckless. They don't follow traffic safety laws like bikers do. They don't look twice to save your life. They don't care."

Offensive to drivers? Sure. But that's not your niche. If you're neutral, you don't spark emotions. If you're politically conservative or liberal, let that come across if you and your niche have those views in common. Like I said in Chapter 5, you're going to make some people *really* like you while others abandon your community entirely. It may be worth it. Your call.

Attractive characters stand on a future-based cause. Think an us-versus-them scenario. Who do you fight for? What are they trying to accomplish? What problem can you help them defeat?

For me, I empower lawyers who've been taken advantage of by marketing companies. I help them learn how to better market their law firms so they can have a fighting chance.

The best non-lawyer example I've ever seen of future-based causes? Successful presidential campaigns. Go back to 1992 and look at election winners' slogans.

In 2016, Donald Trump's, "Make America Great Again," beat Hillary Clinton's, "I'm With Her."

In 2008, Barack Obama's, "Hope and Change," beat John McCain's, "Country First."

In 1996, Bill Clinton's, "Building a Bridge to the 21st Century," beat Bob Dole's, "The Better Man for a Better America."

Dole's slogan made a rookie marketing mistake—talking about yourself in your marketing.

In 1992, Bill Clinton's, "Don't Stop Thinking About Tomorrow," beat George Bush's, "Kinder, Gentler Nation."

Every single winner's slogan is talking about the future. Future-based causes play well with us-versus-them stands. For me, I lead attorneys on a crusade to take back control of their marketing from all the crappy marketing companies. See what I'm doing? I put the lawyers against the marketing companies, and I stand on the lawyers' side.

Create a rallying cry around your law firm, just like sports teams and political parties. Everybody wants to feel like they belong. These emotions solidify you as the leader of your movement.

If you're a personal injury attorney, you can take a stand against bad motorists or insurance companies. Or both. As long as you're on the victims' side, your cause can be you against everybody. Motorcycle riders already dislike insurance companies. Claims agents notoriously dismiss and even *blame* bikers. "I'm sorry, but you assumed a certain amount of risk when you rode that motorcycle."

Your future-based causes can be new laws that protect riders and better, fairer policies from insurance companies. If you practice family law, you can stand against unfair child support laws. Or you can be against the ex-spouse and berate "these deadbeat dads we're all so sick and tired of" in your videos.

For criminal defense, you can be against the criminal justice system. You can be against drug manufacturers. You can be against over-prescribing doctors. Meanwhile, you fight to change laws and hold the pill-pushers accountable.

"It's not your family member's fault," you might say in a video. "I blame the drug manufacturers and all these irresponsible pain clinics. And I'm pushing for rehabilitation over jail time."

If you're an Intellectual Property attorney, you can be against patent trolls. And your future-based cause is to protect IP owners so the patent trolls can't sue, make ridiculous amounts of money, and steal people's ideas.

For bankruptcy law, rally against bill collectors, creditors, or predatory lenders. Talk about making it easier to pay off debts.

If you're an immigration attorney, it's easy to stand against the government, ICE, or a political party behind unfavorable immigration laws. Your future-based cause might be more lenient immigration laws, fairer trials, and better treatment.

If you're an employment lawyer, you can be against the employers in a certain industry, or even one specific employer. Stand up for federal government employees, for example. Or talk about how much you hate office "good old boys'" clubs. In this case, you advocate reporting and protecting against workplace harassment and discrimination.

By this point, I'm sure your brain is overflowing with ideas. So many, in fact, that you don't know where to start. You've got your video persona down—you're an attractive character leading a movement. Now, you need a process to generate high quality video ideas in as little time as possible and with the least amount of effort.

When I first started recording videos, I spent twenty to thirty minutes in front of my computer every day trying to come up with a topic. *I have to record this video right now, and I have no idea what to talk about!* Talk about stress I didn't need.

Now I have a running list of high-value content ideas so I don't have to worry. I just pick a topic off my list and hit record. It's like playing golf. When I agonize over my swing, I play terribly. I miss every fairway, overshoot every green, and miss even two-foot putts. When I don't overthink it, I just hit the ball. I get the occasional birdie instead of double and triple bogeys every hole. When you rack your brain for video ideas, you get frustrated, your content is forced, and you end up in the weeds.

To build your high quality video ideas list, start by looking at your own website. Look at every practice area. Scan any blog posts you've already published. Make a note of every topic you've already covered in your ideas document (I use Evernote to keep track).

Next, think about every client you've ever had. Every consultation. Write down every frequently asked question you can think of for each of your practice areas. If you're a personal injury lawyer, go to your car accident page and write down all the questions prospects, leads, and clients ask about car accidents. Same goes for motorcycle accidents, construction accidents, slip and fall, and premises liability.

Make topics related to your niche your highest priority. Frequently asked questions are my favorite. You probably already know the answer (meaning you won't need to do any research or preparation) *and* you know people actually want to know the answer.

Turn every single question into a video. No catch-alls like, "Twenty Questions About Alimony, Answered." One question, one video. Period. For each video, spin your answers into a story. Repurpose a client's story or talk about something that happened to another attorney's client. Either way, change the details so you don't breach client confidentiality.

Next, head over to www.AttorneyKeywords.com. This is a tool that helps you generate search engine optimized titles to help you reach as many people in your niche as possible. It's great to have a giant content library, but it's even better to help the masses *find* it. www.AttorneyKeywords.com makes that happen. This will come in handy when you publish on YouTube (owned by Google) or transcribe your videos and post them as blog articles. (More on blogging later.) All you have to do is get your free trial and sign up for an attorney profile. You can customize and tailor everything to your niche. Key in your frequently asked questions (and other ideas), and the software generates unlimited title ideas.

Viewer-Friendly Content, Creator-Friendly Process

Every video I publish benefits the viewer. If my content *isn't* good—if it's self-serving or self-promotional—nobody pays attention. People unsubscribe from my list. That's why I don't sell or pitch. You'll *never* hear me say, "If you need help marketing your law firm, call me today!" The second I do that, all my credibility as an authority goes out the window. So what do I say instead?

"Do you have questions related to this video? Shoot me an email."

It's like Angela's free strategy session offer. It's not intimidating. It doesn't set off any alarms. People don't click away from my video thinking, *Oh God, he's gonna try to sell me something...* High value. No pitching. No selling.

Also, remember who your audience is *not*. They're not lawyers! Lawyers are guilty of *talking* like lawyers. Don't get technical and start listing off statutes or calling out cases from memory. Just tell a story and talk like a real person. How do you chat with non-lawyer friends over a beer at the bar? That's the tone (and the vocabulary) of a high value video.

And keep your videos short. A few weeks ago, an attorney sent me his first attempt at video. I looked at the time. *One hour.* I watched for two minutes, got bored, and turned it off. Now, he's my client. The average person has such a short attention span. Say what you have to say in two to five minutes, *no more*.

Simple and finished is better than complex and incomplete. You don't have to spend thousands of dollars setting up an in-office recording studio. All you need is your smartphone, a tripod, and maybe a lavalier microphone (lavalier mics clip to your shirt and plug into your smartphone). Good mic means good audio. If people can't hear you...well, what's the point?

Always turn your phone sideways when you strap it onto your tripod. Otherwise your viewers will be distracted by those annoying black bars. It's like when your TV defaults to widescreen instead of full screen.

But again, *done* is better than perfect. The tripod and mic shouldn't cost more than thirty or forty bucks, but if you don't want to wait, by all means, start today using your computer's built-in webcam. Or just hold the phone in your hand! You're still going to be ahead of your competition as long as you're consistently putting up content. A *good* system you follow is better than the *best* system you don't.

When should you shoot your videos? Whenever you can find the time during daylight hours. Natural lighting is your best source of light. Whether first thing after sunrise, just before dusk, or anywhere in between, find five minutes in front of a window. Film with you *facing* the window versus you sitting or standing in front of a window. Otherwise, you'll appear dark, and light from the window makes it hard to see you.

For your first three or four videos, you may need to set aside more like twenty or thirty minutes. You don't want to feel rushed and frustrated as you're trying to figure out how much light you need, how to turn on your mic, or where to set your tripod. Once you've done a few videos and you're recording every day, you'll get in the groove and it won't take you that long.

Pick a time to film that's convenient for you. That's why your smartphone matters. The most convenient time may not be when you're at your computer, or even at your office. And yes, it has to be you in these videos. *You* are the star of your videos. Not an associate or an assistant. If that person leaves your firm, you've got yourself one useless video library. You're the authority—the leader. You know what attractive characters *don't* do? Hide behind their employees.

Once your videos go live on YouTube and in your Facebook group, it's time to leverage the traffic you own—your email list. But before you email today's video to your community, get that video transcribed. You're not going to *just* email the transcription—first, publish your cleaned up transcription along with the video on your law firm's blog.

For attorneys, blogging is imperative. When organic or paid traffic finds your website—which you don't control, but *do* want—you want them sticking around for a while. And a blog with hundreds of relevant, easy-to-read, high value articles create the same binge effect as your YouTube channel. And when you email today's video to your community, where do you send them? *Your blog*.

(Are you panicking because you don't have a blog yet? Relax. You can create one on your law firm's official website. That way, all of your content is on a single domain. Way too many lawyers publish their blogs as separate websites, meaning visitors have to *leave* the firm's website to read them—big mistake. Keep potential clients on your official site where they can contact you by email, complete an intake form, or even speak directly with your team.)

Whether they find you on Google or click your email link, potential clients get a different feel from your blog than the rest of your website. Most sections of your law firm's site will be strictly informational. They list the types of cases you handle along with your bio and contact information—possibly client testimonials as well. But like your videos, your articles give clients a sense of your personality, your commitment and passion, and your mastery of the law. After all, they're cleaned up video transcriptions!

Want another reason to syndicate videos to your blog? *Beat Google at their own game*. Fresh, high quality content skyrockets your website to the top of Google search results. Your competition? Their law firm's stale blog features the Duke lacrosse case—back when it was front page news!

Because you've got a relevant video topics list (and therefore blog topics list), traffic won't get turned off by the usual suspects. For example, most personal injury and criminal defense attorneys use their "blogs" to talk about local accidents and crimes. But your niche will be thinking, *If it doesn't affect me, I couldn't care less.*

And whatever you do, do not—repeat, DO NOT—publish your articles as long blocks of uninterrupted text. They're *unbearable* to read. I once got an attorney's newsletter in my mail that featured a wall of text with zero paragraph breaks about some community safety award. I couldn't read it. Into the recycling bin it went.

When you publish your daily content as both videos *and* articles, you're all set for email. You're not going to copy-and-paste the entire article in your emails, of course. People don't read novels. Plus, we get, what, two hundred emails per day on average? Just lift three or four lines from the beginning of your video as a teaser, highlighting the value. That's it. That's all you need to win a click. Then people go watch your video, and the video does the hard work.

Don't worry about spamming people. Trust me. I email *thousands* of lawyers every single day. My emails get about a 20% open rate every time. Now, it's not the same 20% opening them every day. So, if I want *most* lawyers on my list to read my blog or watch my videos sometime in the next week, daily emails are my one and only hope. Once again, the keyword is *daily*. Forget this every other day or every third day stuff. That's not enough to create that crucial top of mind awareness. Most people I talk to don't even realize I email them every single day. You're actually reaching people every third, fourth, or fifth day.

If your emails are high value, you'll have a very, very low unsubscribe rate. And you'll also have a very, very low number of people writing back and demanding you stop emailing them.

You know what I *have* received? Dozens of emails telling me how much lawyers love my content and look forward to my emails. One lawyer even said, "Hey, I didn't get an email from you today." They did, of course, but it had gotten buried in their inbox. It just goes to show people don't realize I'm sending an email literally *every single day*.

When you provide value via email, people are happy to visit your other channels. So drive them there! At the bottom of your email, link to your Facebook community, YouTube, and other social media platforms like Instagram or LinkedIn. Maybe even drive people to your Google Reviews!

Your daily content syndication system matters because most people aren't ready to hire you on the spot. That's why, when you go to Amazon and search "toasters" but don't buy, you see toaster ads on every website for the next three weeks. Online retailers know that people don't always buy the first time, but there's a lot of money to be made in that follow up.

When lawyers contact me asking about my services, it's not after the first email. Or the tenth. It's more like after thirty to fifty emails. *That* is when I'm perceived as the authority. And keep in mind, they're not seeing all fifty emails from me. Maybe only ten or fewer.

So, let's see what a winning email looks like.

"Loud Pipes Save Lives" - Is It True? ⊅

████ ████ via s4.asa1.acemsa1.com   Sat, Sep 8, 1:07 PM ☆ ↰ ⋮
to andy+523647 ▾

INJURY LAW

The saying "Loud Pipes Save Lives" is based on the notion that the louder your exhaust pipes are, the more likely it is that other motorists will hear you...which could potentially prevent a collision.

While this may be a common saying, is there any truth to it?

Check out this video to reveal the surprising answer...

Watch Now >> https://youtu.be/████████

Questions? Reply to this email or give me a call at (████████) and I'll point you in the right direction.

Stay safe,

████ ████

Join the FREE ████ ████ ████ ████ ████ for daily content related to all things motorcycles in the state of Georgia.

My personal injury attorney client sent this email. See that subject line?

Loud Pipes Save Lives. Is It True?

Your subject line always evokes curiosity or provides value. Capture attention in half a second, or that email never gets opened. If you ride motorcycles, you've heard the phrase, "Loud pipes save lives." Most bikers are intrigued because this lawyer is challenging conventional biker wisdom. What if a loud bike *isn't* a safety feature? Instant curiosity.

What do you notice about the body of the email? You don't see a 2,000-word dissertation. Just a short intro. A teaser, basically. The reader shouldn't be able to answer the question by reading the email. We're just trying to get people to click the link. Once again, don't pitch. Not in the video, and not in the email. At the bottom, notice what the attorney wrote.

Questions? Reply to this email or give me a call, and I'll point you in the right direction.

If one email recipient has a case, *boom*. There's your consultation. Even if you don't hear back from anyone, chances are a lot of people getting your emails will end up in your Facebook group. Then people see your content in two places. You're also posting your videos in your Facebook group every day, right? Another winning email subject line is the reliable how-to.

In the world of lawyer marketing, any review is usually better than no review.

If your law firm lacks reviews from your previous clients, other prospective clients may be hesitant to work with you.

Or worse, they may opt to work with another law firm with established reviews on Google or Facebook...

If you just can't get your clients to leave reviews for your firm, is there another alternative that can be used?

Fortunately, I have seen this case all too often, and I have created a video that will answer this question.

Check it out!

https://youtu.be/iGfYTDhsOSY

Thanks,

Andy Stickel

Repetition through syndication is *huge*. We're trying to get you past that gold standard of thirty touchpoints to establish top of mind awareness. This system makes your job much, much easier.

And if you're providing value—which you are—you can get to thirty touches in a couple of weeks, especially if a lot of people open your emails. Take the "loud pipes save lives" example. The open rate for that email is 56.98%. The legal industry average open rate? Only 22.62%. That's two-and-a-half times better than the standard. Keep in mind, he's sending *daily* emails! His click through rate? The percentage of people who click the link to watch his video is 29.07%. The average click through rate for the legal industry is 3%. That's *ten times* higher. What about unsubscribes? My client only lost one subscriber in the month leading up to that email. That's 0.1%. The legal industry unsubscribe rate is 0.23%, so his is 43% *lower* than average.[1]

Want to achieve these same numbers? Follow all the steps of my system, from video topic generation to recordings tips to email best practices. Provide a ton of value. It all adds up to a much better open rate, a much better click through rate, and a much lower unsubscribe rate.

Who would have thought that daily emails would work this well? Not most lawyers. They're afraid to email every day because they think they're going to annoy people. And they probably will because they're not sending the right *kind* of emails.

When your content syndicates across your group, your blog, and all the other social media platforms, what happens? You get leads. A *lot* of them.

There's a wrong way to market on social media, a wrong way to record videos, and a wrong way to send emails. There's also a wrong way to convert leads into clients. But that means there's also a *right* way. Let me show you both.

Chapter 7
Sealing the Deal

Boldly Go Where No Lawyer Has Gone Before

There has never been a law firm that succeeded without sales.

Okay, so I'm loosely paraphrasing billionaire Mark Cuban.[1] In any case, he's right. Let's say you've picked the most profitable niche. You've created bait that converts video ad viewers into subscribers and group members. People open your emails like crazy and comment on every single one of your daily Facebook group posts. *You're just THAT good.* Then it happens. Somebody in your group signals to you. It's time.

Remember the motorcycle accident video in the Atlanta personal injury attorney's group? My client created an environment where the first thing people do after an accident is post about it in the Facebook group.

My client did everything right—up until he posted that comment. Now, don't get the idea I'm taking a dig at him. I'm not. He made a mistake, and it could be my fault, as I told him to avoid pitching as much as possible. So let's simply turn that mistake into an extremely profitable sales lesson.

So, what exactly went wrong? In that paragraph, all the lawyer did was give information. Now, providing value is great! But he offered *no* reason to contact his office to request legal representation. I noticed this right away and texted my client.

9:33

> **Morning!** Did you ever talk to that guy that was in the accident yesterday? Wasn't sure if that Would turn into a case. Regardless, that's exactly what we're looking for.

No he never reached out after my comment. Did want to look pushy. Who knows he may still do so.

> Maybe direct message him? "One more thing I forgot...you should blah blah blah". Offer to review his insurance policy for him for free or something?

Good thought. Will do.

iMessage

The guy had a good case, and he posted in the group immediately. No chance he had a lawyer by the time he posted that video. All my client had to do was reel him in. But he didn't.

At this point, you might be thinking, *Wait a minute, Andy. What about all that talk in the last chapter about not coming across as salesy? I thought I wasn't supposed to tell people to "call today"?*

I believe in *asking* for the sale, not *telling* people to buy. Big difference. One is helpful, one is salesy. You'd be surprised how many cases you've missed out on because you didn't want to look pushy (or in the case of my fishing metaphor, "pully").

Remember, in business, sales is the *only* thing that matters. Yes, you're a fantastic lawyer, but that's not why people hire you. Clients want *you* to represent them because they're convinced you're the *best* lawyer for them. Don't worry—I've never met a lawyer who couldn't improve their sales skills, and that's exactly what you're about to do.

I most often talk to lawyers whose retention rate is 25% to 35%. Yours probably is, too. Imagine if you could bump that up to 50% or 65%. Already there? Great! Bump your rate from 50% up to 75%— or higher. For most law firms, adding as few as two or three new cases a month is a big deal.

The best part? Skyrocketing your retention rate is simple. *Crazy* simple, actually. All you have to adjust is how you talk to the leads you're generating. And you *don't* have to pump more cash into Facebook to increase volume. I'm going to show you quick techniques that will allow you to get more people to hire your firm.

Let's start with how you interact with your niche community when people post. Don't just toss out the tips like the attorney above did. If you were in his shoes, you would've commented on the motorcycle accident video and asked a lot of questions or offered to provide some sort of free help. All you're trying to do is start a dialogue.

The attorney and I wrote three comment scripts he can use the next time someone posts about an accident or injury.

"If you want, send me over your insurance policy information. I'll review it, and make sure everything looks good."

"Send me over the police report. Take a picture with your phone. I'll take a look and see if there's anything that jumps out at me, or if there's anything you need to know."

"I can make sure that you're prepared to talk to the adjuster and all that kind of stuff."

Once your lead reaches out to you, turn your private chat into a mini-consultation. You have a few different choices for what to say next. Notice the authoritative tone in all three comments? Remember what Jay Abraham taught us. People need to be led. They *want* to be led. So, *lead*. Helping a frazzled citizen take their next legal steps is valuable in and of itself. Don't kill your authority at the last second by backing away from the sale, or your leads will, too.

Hold on, Andy, you're thinking. *Haven't you been saying that providing free value creates authority, credibility, and top of mind awareness? And that all leads to more clients?*

You're right. I have. But you know what else is valuable besides free tips? *Asking for the sale.* Back away from the opportunity to close a client, and you're basically saying, "Look, I'm just here to give free legal advice. I'm not confident enough to tell you to hire my law firm. I'm not even qualified." That's one message you *never* want to send.

So, what do you do instead? When your lead replies with the information, *ask for the sale*. Ask boldly. Directly. Unabashedly.

"Looking at this, here's what I see. I see that if you want, we could definitely try to get some of these medical bills covered for you. Do you want me to help you with that?"

What would an injured, wrecked biker say to that? What would just about *any* potential client say?

"Yes, absolutely. Thank you."

Boom. Sold. You've got a client. Let your office work out the details.

When you're closing leads from your social media group, stop giving tips. That's how you get *leads*, not *clients*. See the difference? Otherwise, you'll be like the attorney before my sales coaching. He gave free tips at the wrong time. The potential client hired another lawyer, who probably won a handsome settlement and bought a yacht. Lesson learned.

I'm giving you a whole new way to think about sales. If you do it right, selling *is* providing value. You don't tell members of your group, "If you've been injured, let's get a consultation on my schedule." That's ripped straight from daytime local TV ads.

Offer to take a quick look at an insurance policy or police report, and your leads run *to* the transaction. Not away from it. All you have to do is start a dialogue. Ask questions, so they always have to respond. Avoid a cold sales pitch. That's not an invitation. My strategy is.

"Just Try It For Two Months"

By now you've hit the lead-generating jackpot. You're active in your social media community, and user-generated content creates even more engagement. You're running video ads. You email potential clients every day. And people wander—to your other social media profiles, to your group, and to your website.

But we all know there's another way people find you. Not everyone takes the time for a Facebook group post (or they're not in the group). Not everyone finds your website on Google and fills out your contact form. What do a lot of people do? Pick up the phone.

Remember the last time you called a business trying to reach customer service? What happened? You didn't hear a real, live human. You got a prerecorded or robotic voice that said, "Hi, you've reached _____. Press one for _____. Press two for _____. Press three for _____. Press four for _____."

How happy were you when you heard this menu?

Oh man, I'm so happy I get to talk to this machine! It gets me. It knows what I need. It always answers my problems. It solves all my issues. I feel like this machine cares about me!

Nope. Nobody thinks that. Ever. Not when they call customer service, and not when they call your law firm.

I recently advised a client to replace his phone tree with a real, life person.

"There's no way that matters," he said. "People don't care. They're happy to listen to all the options to get the right person on the other end."

"Just try it for two months. If you do it, and it doesn't drastically increase your intake, I will pay for your phone tree system for the next six months."

"You've got yourself a deal."

Two months later, his intake had doubled. But that wasn't the wild part. When we looked over his phone records, we discovered that his phone call volume had NOT increased. The only thing he did was replace a machine with a human. I guarantee you one thing—he now wishes he'd dumped the call tree menu years ago! In fact, he sent me this email:

I tested the new answering service for two months, and it seems to work well. Our intake has gone from 27 new clients in October and November to 55 new clients in December and January. But the number of phone calls didn't increase.

Think about an emergency situation. Maybe you just got served divorce papers while your spouse is out of town on business. Imagine how you feel. Angry, maybe. Devastated, probably. Vulnerable, definitely. What do you do? And do you want to talk to a machine or a human being?

If you're a sole practitioner, find an answering service. If it's at all possible, you need to have your phone answered by a live person—24/7. That means any time of day or night, all year round, when your potential clients call you, they get a real, live human being. Ask your colleagues what service they use. It's not expensive, not much more than $200 a month. I guarantee it'll be worth it. You'll get more cases which will more than pay for your answering service investment.

Treat every lead as urgent. Potential clients don't want to leave a message or wait days to hear back from an attorney—they want help with their legal matter *right away*.

If you have an employee who answers the phone at your law firm— usually the receptionist—*thoroughly* train them to handle leads properly. They have to get across to the lead that they understand the urgency of the situation.

If a lawyer isn't available to speak to the lead *literally right now*, the receptionist first should apologize. Get contact information. Then give a specific time when to expect a return call. That same day, of course. If your receptionist lets the call go to voicemail, what would've been your case now belongs to a competitor. Most people won't waste fifteen seconds on a voicemail. They've got an urgent problem to solve, and they'll keep calling your competitors until they get an answer.

Face-to-Face Selling in Five Easy Steps

Whether you're talking to leads on social media or over the phone, sooner or later, you'll have in-person consultations. Too many cases get lost at this final step, after the potential client spent time and effort to get in front of you. Say the wrong thing at the wrong time to a person's face, and off they go to your competitor's office. And if the lead is sold on hiring *a* lawyer, just not you, your competitor wins a case without even having to work for it. Sucks, doesn't it?

Most lawyers have trouble closing deals because they're not trained salespeople. Remember that course in law school that taught you how to sell? Don't worry—none of your competitors do either! So pat yourself on the back, because you're about to get a huge leg up on them. Every professional salesperson knows that people remember not what you *say*, but how you make them *feel*.

Remember Angela Langlock's advice about acting *too* professional? In a selling situation, talking like a lawyer turns people off. When you talk to a potential client, you're selling *emotions*, not legal services. You're selling the relief that they won't lose their kids, that they'll have money for their medical bills, or that they won't go to jail. You're going to get the IRS off their backs or sue that employee who poached their customers. Trigger these emotions, and you're hired. Who cares about all those fancy awards and plaques on your wall? Not the person seated across from you. Remember, it's not about you—it's about the benefits of hiring you.

It's a fact of human psychology that we buy on emotion then logically justify the transaction afterward. For example, people buy brand new cars because they fall in love with them. When they get home, they have to justify the purchase to their spouse or themselves. They say, "But it's got great gas mileage, and there's plenty of room for the kids."

If you make a potential client feel as comforted as possible—that *their* problems are now *your* problems—congratulations! *You're hired.*

Sales trainer Ryan Stewman taught me a simple five-step sales process that I share with every client—and now, with *you*. Learn these steps, follow them every time, and I guarantee you'll increase your sales.

Step one, get clients talking. You're already doing this when you send leads a direct message on social media. But don't stop there. When a lead comes in for a consultation, ask, "What made you choose to come in today?" Then establish that you're going to have an honest and fair conversation. Most people have never hired a lawyer and they probably don't trust you.

This opener gets prospective clients talking immediately about their legal issue—their pain. You also want to establish that they made the *right* choice, which people struggle to do all the time. (If you need proof, just ask your spouse where they want to go for dinner tonight.)

Step two, shut up and listen. Let prospective clients answer your question in as much detail as possible. Fight the urge to interrupt with your own thoughts or opinions for now—just let them talk. The more you talk, the less you make. You *want* potential clients to tell you every problem they've ever had, because people tell their problems to those they trust. The more they tell you, the more they trust you.

Take notes as they're talking. Identify their pain points—what are their worries, goals, and fears? What do they believe will happen if they don't hire an attorney?

Once they finish, on to **step three**—ask deeper questions. Jump in and ask open-ended questions about their pain points to get them talking again. Gently open up these sore spots. Say, "To learn how I can best help you, I'm going to ask you some difficult questions, but I need you to answer honestly. If you have any questions for me, feel free to interrupt and I'll answer honestly as well. Does that sound fair?"

For example, let's say you're talking to a parent preparing to file for divorce. One of their biggest pain points may be the fear of losing their children in a custody battle. Let them get these thoughts, worries, and fears off of their chest.

Step four, figure out the real problem. Every client's real problem is specific to them. You want to bring it out in the open so you can address it. Maybe your potential client's spouse cheated, but they're worried about having money to support themselves. You need to know this. Maybe they can't pay all the bills on their own, but their primary concern is keeping their home. You need to know. Maybe their child has a brain injury, so they need medical care more than a large settlement. Ask questions to find out. You need to know their *specific* pain is so you can offer to solve it. If you go to the dentist with a toothache, they don't immediately treat your whole mouth with fluoride. They figure out the actual problem, *then* they deal with the tooth that hurts. Don't just blunder into a sales pitch for your firm. Wait until you have enough information, and even then, drape your ask in value.

And finally, once you've identified their pain, you want to get permission to help them—**step five**. By this point, you should have a better understanding of why they need your legal services. Make it clear to them that you understand *exactly* what they need from you by restating their pain points and offering legal assistance.

For example, you could say, "I know this is your first DUI and you're scared, but I can fight to keep you out of jail. I've helped many people in your exact situation. Would you like my help?" Or, "I understand medical bills are piling up, and you're scared. I know exactly how to deal with the insurance companies in this situation. Would you like me to help you with this?" Or, "I understand that you are worried about losing primary custody of your children, but I can help you prevent this outcome."

Show the client that you listened, you understand their pain, and you know how to achieve the outcome they want. This simple technique will make the prospective client feel safe with you. At this point, some people are going to say yes, and that's all it takes. Others will want to think about it because they're afraid of lawyers. If you truly believe that the service you provide helps people, it's your moral obligation to move them to hire you. To do that, you're going to incentivize them to commit today. Not tomorrow. Not next week. Not after they "think it over." *Today.*

Say something like, "If you hire us today, I will immediately file this motion today so you can see your kids soon." Or, "If you decide to hire us right now, I'll call your insurance company. I'll demand payment today so you can get your medical bills paid."

Whatever you can do to give the client instant gratification, do it. Feel free to get as creative as possible. If you're a criminal defense attorney, you could say, "Hire us today, and not only will we handle your DUI, but I'll handle your DMV hearing at no charge. I'll even work to get you a special license so you can still drive to and from work."

If you're a personal injury lawyer, say, "Hire us today, and we'll make appointments for you with the doctors we trust. They only get paid after your case is over, so you can get the help you need today."

In both examples, I use the "so you can" statement, which attaches a benefit to your immediate action with the bonus. If you practice this simple method and don't deviate, your close ratio will increase. Guaranteed.

That said, these five steps aren't the *only* way to increase your intake. I also teach experienced lawyers a sophisticated sales strategy I learned from Russell Brunson. If you're ready for an advanced lesson on taking your consultations to the next level, then I'm ready to teach.

How to Sell an iPhone for $10,000

Remember that time a prospect told you they had no money? *Which one?* you're thinking. *There were so many.*

Even high-quality leads with strong cases tell you, "I need legal advice, but I can't afford legal services." Don't believe this lie. People will find money for an attorney if it's their one and only shot at achieving their desired outcome. (Most of the time, it is.) So, show these leads why they can't afford *not* to hire your law firm.

I recently had a call with a criminal defense attorney. We'd just started working together because he was so frustrated with his marketing.

"I'm tired of getting outbid." He vented. "I'm losing clients to these lower priced firms. They'll do a DUI for $500. It's a volume-based business."

"You have this problem because you've commoditized yourself."

"I've what?"

"You offer a widely available service. A DUI with your firm? Probably interchangeable with the other guys' offer, but you charge more. No offense, but even though you're way more hands-on with your clients, they don't know that up front."

"Fair enough." He nodded slowly. "What can we do about it?"

"Since price is a stopping point for clients, we're going to decommotidize your legal services. It's an advanced strategy, but I think you're ready for it. After all, there's no strategic advantage to be the second lowest price. If you're going to compete on price, you either have to be the absolute cheapest, or you have to be the most expensive. But the reality is, price isn't a good thing to compete over."

"I can see that. Tell me about this advanced strategy of yours."

"We want to make sure that when you're competing, you're competing as a standalone. In other words, you're not competing with *anyone*. It's just you. You're not a commodity anymore."

"Go on."

"Let's create a special *offer*. So, when someone comes to you, they hire you because you are the authority. You give the best service they literally can't get anywhere else."

"Let's do it. Just tell me how."

Most lawyers don't understand the idea of "the offer." It's not your fault—once again, no law school teaches it! Before I explain *how* to decommoditize your law firm and design your one-of-a-kind legal services offer, let's look at *what* an offer actually is.

Russell Brunson first explained the concept to me with a wild example—how he can sell an iPhone for $10,000. It's the perfect illustration. You can buy iPhones pretty much anywhere smartphones are sold—online, in stores, at auction, on Craigslist. When you buy an iPhone, you choose a carrier with the best price, whether that's Sprint, T-Mobile, Verizon, or whoever. If you can buy the *same* product anywhere, all sellers have to compete on is price. So, how would you sell an iPhone for $10,000?

The secret is the offer. For example, let's say I wanted to sell lawyers an iPhone for $10,000. (This is just an example. I'm not selling an iPhone. Don't email me asking about unlimited data plans.)

The first thing you get is the phone itself, which has a retail value of $997. Everybody else is selling the iPhone, too, so what else can I offer to up the value? What if I took every training video I've ever created and pre-loaded them into the phone's media section? Based on what my courses and trainings sell for separately, we're talking $20,000 worth of value, easy.

What else? I could install an app called Voxer. It's basically a walkie-talkie that connects to my iPhone. Any time you have a law firm marketing question, pull out your phone, hit the Voxer button, and connect directly to my phone. I charge coaching clients $30,000 per year for this level of instant access to me.

I'd also go into the iPhone web browser and bookmark my top twenty-five recommended marketing vendors. That way, you can quickly build a team to get everything done for you. Need a graphic designer? Done. Need a chat box installed on your website? My research has a $2,000 value.

Lastly, I would open up the phone's calendar app, add twelve appointments with me, and sync them to both of our calendars. You'd get monthly appointments with me where I'm your Chief Marketing Officer for one year. I walk you and your team through your entire marketing strategy. I charge clients $60,000 a year for this service.

What's the total value of my hypothetical iPhone offer? The phone itself, trainings and courses, instant Q&A, marketing vendor list, and CMO access for a year totals $112,000. But I'm going to sell you this entire package for one payment of $10,000. If I really offered this, I guarantee you I'd have to stock up on iPhones—in bulk.

Let's review exactly *how* I designed this hypothetical offer. I took a commodity product—a smartphone—and created a unique product that you can't get at AT&T. You can't get it *anywhere else* for *any* amount of money. So, how would, say, a personal injury attorney design an irresistible offer like this?

If you're a personal injury attorney, all you've had to compete on up to this point is experience. That's if you lower your contingency fee, which is a bad idea. You can't give coupons or offer discounts either. Instead, you take services you provide anyway and turn them into offers. The first thing clients receive is your undivided personal attention. What's the value? Assign one. Say something like, "On average, I work on personal injury cases for three hundred hours, and my rate is $250 an hour. You'll also receive the attention of my entire staff. That's a combined value of over $75,000."

Pile on the value. Say, "You're going to have medical concerns. We will provide exclusive medical concierge service. We'll connect you with the right physical therapist and chiropractor to suit your needs. We will put you in touch with all the doctors we trust. We'll make sure you get your appointments quickly. And we'll ensure all payment arrangements are taken care of for you."

Many injury attorneys that I know do this anyway, but how many other personal injury attorneys package it like this? And how many assign a value to it?

Talk about any other legal experts you'll engage with on your client's behalf. Say, "You're also going to get our team of legal experts. I've been a trial lawyer for two decades now. Should your case go to trial, you need to know which legal experts to consult with and which do well with juries. More importantly, you need to know which ones to avoid. I've put together the dream team of legal experts."

Now, take a cue from my hypothetical offer. Say, "If you retain our firm, we're also going to install an app on your phone called Voxer. It links to an app on my phone. That way, if you have questions, all you have to do is pull out your phone, press a button, and talk like it's a walkie talkie. It doesn't matter if it's two o'clock in the morning. I'm here for you. As soon as I see your message, you'll get a reply."

Feel free to be creative, too. For example, as an outside the box idea, maybe offer to help clients set up a GoFundMe campaign to help pay their bills while the case is going on. Does it matter if other attorneys provide similar (or identical) services and resources? Nope. Because you're the first to package them in a unique offer and assign a high value. Again, it doesn't matter if you were going to offer all of this anyway. We sell based on emotions, not logic, because that's how people buy. Let your competition fight with facts while you win with feelings—on social media, over the phone, and in person.

Handling the Ultimate Objection

Have you ever heard a potential client say, "I need a lawyer, but I don't have any money"? Let me teach you a simple way to handle this objection. First of all, understand that nobody wants to spend money. But nobody expects to a lawyer to work for free either. So, you have to accept that people have money even if claim they don't. People have credit cards. They can get loans. They can ask family members for money if necessary. The next time you get the "I'm broke" objection, say, "Isn't that why you're here in the first place?" For example, if someone approaches you about handling their DUI, you can say, "How do you plan to make money if you can't drive a car, lose your job, and get evicted?" If you're a family law attorney, say to the disgruntled spouse seeking child support, "How will you make sure you're getting the child support you need and deserve if you don't have a lawyer? You're simply not going to achieve that result without representation, whether it's our firm or another. It's much cheaper now. " If you're a bankruptcy attorney, you could say, "How will you fix your credit and buy a home for your family one day if you don't hire a lawyer to help you with your debt now?" And if you're a tax attorney, say, "If you don't hire an attorney to fix your tax problems now, you're going to continue incurring penalties and interest that will far outweigh my fees."

If you don't get the money objection until after you've given your firm's price, start dropping a testimonial in there. Say, "This will cost about $3000 for my firm to represent you. We have a lot of experience with cases like this. We had a client just like you, and here is the result we achieved for him..." Flip the money objection on its head and justify your price immediately, and you're going to have a lot of success.

Now, you know how to ask for the sale. You've got a real person answering your phones (or you will soon). And you've learned an advanced selling strategy that virtually none of your competitors use.

That's not all. Defeat your low-balling competition once and for all with the secret weapon of law firm marketing very few attorneys know about. And unlike my closing strategy in this chapter, it has almost nothing to do with what *you* say—and everything to do with what people say *about you*.

Hold on. How do I control what people say about me? I'm about to show you.

Chapter 8
Make Your Clients Your Best Salespeople

"CEO Sells Books With This One Neat Trick. Publishers HATE Him."

Do you remember the first time you ever shopped on Amazon? For many, that takes us back to the mid or late 1990s. Back when Amazon sold just one thing—books.

Amazon Founder and CEO Jeff Bezos set out to build the world's largest bookstore. But selling hundreds of thousands of different titles wasn't the only advantage Amazon had over your local Barnes & Noble. Bezos changed the way the world shops when he released the reviews submission feature. For the first time, readers could rate and review books *negatively*. Since the dawn of modern publishing, authors and publishers had sold books based only on glowing endorsements. You either had them or you didn't. This one to five-star rating thing hadn't come into play yet. In fact, around the turn of the millennium, Bezos had to *defend* online reviews amid industry backlash.

> We want to make every book available—the good, the bad and the ugly, to let truth loose.[1]

Today, Amazon allows customers to review *every* product they sell. Jeff Bezos is single handedly responsible for changing the way we compare and buy products and services—we read the reviews first. And they're written not by professional critics or reviewers, but by people like you and me. That's *why* we trust them. Almost nine out of ten people give online reviews the same credibility they give personal recommendations.[2]

So, what does all this mean for lawyers? *People are checking you out*. It doesn't matter if you have a Google My Business profile yet or not. (Google My Business is a free tool for businesses to manage their online presence across Google, including Reviews, Search, and Maps.) I've worked with several attorneys who found dozens of client reviews on third-party websites like Avvo and Yelp.

Do your potential clients read these reviews before contacting you? You bet they do. In 2014, Software Advice found that 83% of legal consumers visit online review sites as the first step in their search for an attorney.[3]

Like publishers and sellers on Amazon, I've heard many lawyers complain about reviews and ratings over the years. "They're not fair. What somebody writes online doesn't give the full picture. What's to stop my competitor from writing a fake review and screwing me over?" All valid concerns. But here's the thing. *Everyone* plays by the same rules—even if you don't like them. That's why we need to get your online reputation under control *before* it gets out of control.

Put yourself in your clients' shoes. No one wants to hire an average law firm if they have access to a great one. After all, why dine at Waffle House if you can afford Ruth's Chris Steakhouse? People distinguish one law firm from the rest by reading what that firm's clients had to say about them. *If other people had a good experience with these guys, then surely I will, too.*

Think back to the last time you tried a new restaurant, and you checked out the reviews beforehand. Did the ratings and reviews influence your choice? I'll bet they did. What about the last time you bought something on Amazon and you saw two similar products with similar reviews? How did you choose? Did you buy the product with more reviews? You probably did. When products or services have equal ratings, the one with more reviews wins. This is called "social proof." If people see that lots of other folks had a positive experience with a product or service, they believe they will, too.

Are online reviews a way to add value? Absolutely. Help consumers choose the right law firm—yours—so their case doesn't get eaten alive by the sharks in town. Your daily content matters. Your community engagement matters. But get your online reputation wrong, and even your email subscribers will consume your content all day long—then hire a lawyer with more (or better) reviews. Think about the people who get your name from members of your Facebook group. A great referral, right? Well, maybe. It all depends on your online reviews. The first thing they'll do is look up reviews about you. And if that potential client sees another local attorney with a better online reputation than yours, they've just won that case away from you. You won't even know it happened, because you'll never get a call!

If you've ever relied on word-of-mouth referrals and friends of friends for new clients, rethink that strategy. Smart lawyers welcome reviews and, in fact, convert those reviews into savvy marketing tools. (More on that later.)

Okay, Andy, I get it, reviews matter. But just HOW important are reviews for lawyers?

A client called me recently and said, "The phone's been dead for the last, I don't know, six weeks? What's going on?" The first thing I did was look at their Google My Business profile. Everything was the same—except for a new review. A *negative* one. Boom. Just like that, a five-star average rating dropped down to three-stars. Another client, same phenomenon. A single negative review dropped his five-star average rating down to four. In both instances, the phone stopped ringing when their average rating decreased. Is it any wonder why? According to BrightLocal, if your business averages three stars or fewer, you'd get more clicks if your law firm had *no reviews at all*.[4] And more phone calls, presumably. (More on responding to negative reviews in a minute.)

Like I said, review *quality* isn't the only thing that matters. Your potential clients look for *quantity*. I have a bankruptcy attorney client who ranks high in organic search results. Second place, to be exact. Businesses pay literally thousands of dollars a month for that privilege. So, why wasn't he getting any phone calls? You can guess. His top competitor had fifteen Google reviews, and my client only had five. More reviews, more phone calls. So, I gave my client a homework assignment—get to twenty-five positive reviews. I told him to try sending out an email blast to past clients, or to get on the phone if he had to. And he actually listened to me! Four days later, he had gotten the twenty additional reviews. The following week was the busiest week in the history of his firm. That four days was time well spent. (Later in this chapter, you'll get the exact email template we used.)

I gave another client, a personal injury law firm with several partners, the same assignment. They reached out to past clients, resulting in *forty-six* new Google reviews over a two-week period. Phone calls *quadrupled*. When I asked one of the partners, she said, "Every new client says they were calling because of the great Google reviews." And the best part? They didn't have to spend a dime on ads. They didn't resort to hiring freelancers to post fake positive reviews either.

Want results like this? It's possible. *Likely*, even. First of all, make sure that when people want to leave you a Google Review, they *can*. If you don't have a Google My Business profile, set one up today. If your law firm has multiple locations, you'll need a different profile for each location. It's important that you get a minimum of ten reviews for each location.

And that's the tricky part. The number-one obstacle to get authentic five-star reviews is getting the right people to write them. Let's face it. Leaving a review isn't easy, especially for the non-tech-savvy among us. Something as simple as not remembering their Google password is enough to deter someone from leaving a review, even if they think the world of you. (On the other hand, if somebody is upset with you, they'll do whatever it takes to leave a bad review just so they can give you—and the world—a piece of their mind.)

Even if you won a client ten million dollars in their car accident case, don't expect that to be enough for them to leave you a review. This doesn't mean you did something wrong. Your client didn't write a review like they promised they would because it's just too difficult. Life gets in the way. Work. Kids. Sleep. For someone with a family, *anything* that's not imperative (or extremely enjoyable) ends up at the bottom of the to-do list. It's not because they don't want to leave you a review, and it's got nothing to do with the quality of your service. Maybe your client wondered, *What's in it for me?* And couldn't think of an answer.

Consider this—the only reward your client gets for writing a positive review is the feeling that they've helped you out. When does your client get this feeling? After they write the review like they promised? Nope. In a popular TED Talk, Derek Sivers shares research going back a full century revealing the opposite.[5] If you have a goal (like writing a review) and tell somebody about it, you feel an instant rush of accomplishment. But this makes it less likely that you'll actually follow through.

The best way to overcome this deterrent? Make sure the client knows there's something in it for them if they leave you a review.

Now, relax. I'm not talking about bribery. Instead, offer a small token of your appreciation in exchange for them taking the time to leave you a review. A restaurant, grocery, or coffee gift card works. Notice I didn't say *in exchange for a five-star review*. Now *that's* bribery. Make sure they know you just want a review. (Check state laws and your Bar association rules to make sure that you're in compliance. But you're a lawyer. You can figure out a way to be creative and make this work...your top competitors have!)

Once you give clients the motivation to follow through, make it *super* easy to do so. Eliminate as many clicks as possible. You're going to grab the direct link to write you a review, and share that with clients. Here's how:

If you're using Google My Business, do a Google search for your law firm name. Click "Write a Review." Once that box opens, copy the entire URL (the web address). It's a big, long, scary link isn't it? Don't send that to anybody without shortening it first. Fortunately, free services like those at http://bit.ly help you do just that. Head over there, paste the entire URL, and shorten the link. *That* link is the one you'll send your clients when you ask for their reviews. When the client clicks the link, they're taken directly to the box where they can write you a review. They don't need to find your profile or locate the review button. If the client has a Gmail address, that's even better. When you send your shortened link directly to their Gmail address, this ensures they're already logged in to their Google account. (You can also use this trick to eliminate the steps needed to leave a review on many other review sites, including Yelp and Avvo.)

When someone leaves a Google review, your Gmail address receives a notification. (I should say, *usually* receives a notification. For some reason, notifications don't always end up in your inbox, so check your profile periodically.) When you see a new review, respond immediately. Log in to your Google My Business profile, click on Reviews, and reply with something like, "Thank you for being a valued client!" (Vary every response so potential clients don't see the same copy-and-paste reply on every review.) Not only does a quick response reflect positively on you, but it also shows Google that the review wasn't spam. The last thing you want is Google flagging a glowing five-star review of your firm as spam! If a ton of five-star reviews show up at once on your profile, you bet Google is going to notice. Reply to each one personally to prove you're a real person talking to real clients.

Respond to reviews you receive on other platforms as well. Like Yelp. If you don't get a lot of Yelp reviews, don't ask clients to leave Yelp reviews more often than one client every six to eight weeks. This will ensure every review appears *natural*. Why is this so important on Yelp? Let's say your firm's been around for five years, and you've never gotten any Yelp reviews. Then within a week, you get five Yelp reviews. Something's not right there. Obviously, you asked for reviews. Yelp doesn't *want* you asking clients for reviews. They want reviews to appear naturally. When Yelp's filter detects potentially solicited reviews, the platform filters them out. They get labelled "not recommended." I once had a client fail to listen to my advice. He asked for (and received) fifteen Yelp reviews in one week. Every single one of those reviews got filtered out. Needless to say, the client wasn't happy.

I used to have an advertising partnership with Yelp. Then I saw their dark side. I started warning attorneys about what I felt were Yelp's complicated and shady review practices. Yelp found out, terminated our partnership, and permanently banned me from doing business with them ever again. I am *not* kidding. Whether or not you advertise on Yelp, you should know my opinion about how the platform works.

Besides their mislabeling of completely authentic reviews, Yelp (in my view) uses aggressive sales tactics.

For example, one law firm I know declined to buy advertising from Yelp when their salespeople called. The very next day, all five of the firm's five-star Yelp reviews were filtered and hidden from visitors. Guess what remained visible? The firm's one and only two-star review. Could all of this be coincidence? Sure. But it sure seems suspicious.

I've seen this happen with my clients, too. A personal injury attorney in Los Angeles had several five-star Yelp reviews filtered and only a one-star review showing. They gave no explanation for the filtering. When Yelp called the firm to sell advertising, my client said, "No, because you're hiding our good reviews." Several days later, the rep called back and told the attorney to check his Yelp listing again. My client's five-star reviews were now miraculously unfiltered.

Where there's smoke, there's usually fire. This isn't direct or definitive proof that Yelp is an unethical company. But it does seem more than coincidental. And recently, Yelp made headlines with high-profile lawsuits. In the 2013 case *Yelp v. McMillan*, bankruptcy law attorney Julian McMillan settled with Yelp. Yelp had accused him of posting fake reviews. The report from Ars Technica should serve as a warning to every lawyer:

> Yelp believes that McMillan orchestrated fake reviews on the Yelp page for his bankruptcy law business—an accusation he emphatically denied...

> It seems strange that Yelp would choose to suddenly focus on a small target when presumably fake Yelp reviews are happening on a daily basis across its site.

The San Diego-based attorney had hired Yelp to provide advertising services in 2012 after receiving a cold call from an ad sales representative, but he sued Yelp in small claims court, saying that the terms of that contract were not fulfilled. As he tells it, Yelp sued him essentially as a way to be vindictive.[6]

Beware of Yelp. And don't expect them to meet justice anytime soon. In 2014, 9th U.S. Circuit Court of Appeals Judge Marsha Berzon dismissed two lawsuits against Yelp. Her ruling gave me goosebumps.

[B]usiness owners may deem the posting or order of user reviews as a threat of economic harm, but it is not unlawful for Yelp to post and sequence the reviews...As Yelp has the right to charge for legitimate advertising services, the threat of economic harm that Yelp leveraged is, at most, hard bargaining.[7]

"Hard bargaining." That's BS, in my opinion. It's unfortunate that it was a *lawyer* (Judge Berzon) who gave Yelp so much power over her fellow attorneys' reputations. My advice? If a Yelp representative calls to sell you advertising, even if you aren't interested, don't just say "no." If you aren't buying, stall. Otherwise, you run the risk that Yelp will "sequence" (i.e., hide) your legitimate five-star reviews. Instead, I recommend that you put the salespeople off. Say, "I don't have time to talk now, but could you email me, and we'll schedule something in a few weeks?" or, "Reach back out after I return from my month-long vacation." Do whatever it takes to pause the conversation. I don't feel like saying "No" is worth the risk.

Desperate Times Call For Character Reviews

It's easier for some law practice areas to get reviews than others. A client has no problem going online and thanking their attorney for setting up a trust. But who wants to tell the world about those pesky sexual harassment charges their lawyer got dropped? I get it. But it's no excuse to give up. If your legal services affect clients' private lives or public reputation, guess what? Your competitors probably have trouble getting reviews, too.

If you've logged into your Google My Business profile lately—or ever read online reviews before—you may have noticed what *doesn't* appear anywhere on the Reviews page. "Client." The implication? Your reviews don't necessarily have to come from clients. What if your neighbor or colleague wrote, "This firm cares about their clients. They're extremely knowledgeable. If I was ever in a situation, this is the first firm I'd call."

This review isn't fake. The person isn't lying, claiming you represented them. All they're doing is vouching for your character, your compassion, and your knowledge of the law. It's a solid review, and it does the job. I have no reason to believe Google penalizes character reviews. I've never had a client get in trouble for doing this. That said, client reviews *are* far better and character reviews should be used as a last resort. But if you only have two or three reviews, and one of your competitors has ten or fifteen, who are potential clients going to call? Whether it's family, friends, neighbors, or colleagues, ask and you shall receive. You can even trade reviews with other attorneys you respect who practice different law so you're not in competition.

Liars, Idiots, and How to Talk to Them Both

Every review counts. If you're not able to get clients to leave you reviews, it doesn't mean that you're screwed. If you use the character reviews strategy, don't abuse it. And never stop asking clients to leave you reviews. Because when the negative reviews come (and trust me, they will), you *must* have glowing five-star reviews that prove that reviewer wrong.

If and when someone writes you a negative review, handle it professionally. Don't act like a jerk. My two rules of thumb to remember are one, always respond, and two, always take the high road. That means you apologize. Take responsibility for the misunderstanding. Thank them for their constructive criticism. Don't call the reviewer a liar. And don't call them an idiot (even if they are one). I've seen some lawyers post their own phony reviews to counterbalance the negative review. Don't. Never resort to self-promotional press releases about the situation either. If someone attacks you in a genuinely unfair way, bite the bullet—and remember, a professional reply will raise your law firm in search engine results.

What exactly do I mean by a professional reply? Take a look at the one below. I wrote this for a lawyer who wanted to yell at his client for making wildly false accusations about his law firm. I talked him off the ledge, and this was the result:

> Thank you very much for taking the time to review our law firm. Input and feedback from all our clients is vitally important to us. And we always want client expectations to not only be met, but exceeded. Per your comments, we clearly have had some miscommunication, as there are some inaccuracies in your account of your relationship with our firm. This has obviously led to your frustration for which I greatly apologize. I would like to take the opportunity to discuss the matter with you as soon as possible, so that we can come to a resolution that is to your satisfaction. Please call me at my office as soon as possible or send me an email with a time that works for me to call you. Thank you.

Is the disgruntled client going to call? No way! They're pissed. They just wanted to vent. This response is purely for the thousands (or tens of thousands) of people who will see this review when they're researching my client's firm. Potential clients need to see that you accepted responsibility for the miscommunication. You eagerly desire to make it right. This is the absolute best way to handle negative reviews. Any other response will only make you look guilty.

What about the times when a negative review is *not* from a client? Several family law attorney clients have received these. They won a great result in court, and the ex-spouse now wants revenge. Take the high road, and tell the truth. Get some inspiration from this response I wrote for a client:

> Thank you very much for taking the time to review our law firm. Input and feedback from all our clients is vitally important to us. And we always want client expectations to not only be met, but exceeded. Unfortunately, after checking our records, we have no record of you being a client at our firm. However, we still would like to know why you're so upset. If you would, please contact us at the office so we can do whatever we can to remedy the situation or come to a satisfactory agreement.

Smooth and professional, isn't it? Any potential client who reads a response like this will believe you. But lash out at the reviewer, call them a liar or an idiot, and you only look guilty. Plus, what does that say about your professionalism?

You can't eliminate negative reviews, but you *can* bury them with positive feedback. If nineteen people say you're awesome, and only one reviewer says you suck, very few people pay attention to the detractor. However, if you only have one positive review when you get a negative one, *half* of your online feedback is negative.

A majority of positive reviews can dissuade somebody who wants to assassinate your reputation. If your law firm has twenty, thirty, or forty positive Google reviews and only one negative review, they're less likely to follow through. *Who would believe me?* they'll think. *People will see that everyone else had a great experience, and only one guy didn't. That makes ME the problem.*

Boost Your Reviews (And Search Results) With One Email

Earlier, I told you that your reviews impact your Google ranking. The implication here is that having reviews will *boost* your ranking, which is true. But it happens indirectly. Confused?

Having a ton of five-star reviews does *not* directly increase your Google rankings. However, those reviews *do* increase your click-through rate. An increased click-through rate *does* increase your rankings. One study showed that just having Google reviews increases your website's traffic by an average of 35%![8]

So, how do you go about "boosting" them, and what does that even mean? Well, Google reviews with relevant keywords have had a significant impact on Google rankings in our tests. Now, that doesn't mean that you should tell your clients to "keyword-stuff" their reviews. If possible, ask your clients to include information about the services you've performed for them and in what city and state. I devised a clever trick to get clients to do this, rather than just hoping they'd remember. To do so, send an email like this one:

Dear <Client>,

Thank you so much for taking the time to review our firm. A lot of times, clients are happy with our service, but aren't quite sure what to write in a review. Below are some questions that should give you some ideas, and will make your review more useful for other people that need our services:

- What service did we complete for you?

- Which city or county did we represent you in?

- Did we do a good job?

- What were some of your favorite things about working with us?

- Have we helped you with anything else in the past?

- Did you work with any specific people from our firm you'd like to mention?

- How do we compare to other law firms that you've tried?

- Are there any tips you would offer others about our law firm?

We really appreciate your review. Please provide as much detail as you can, but if you're limited on time, we'd still love a short review.

One and done. Now your clients don't have to come up with something halfway coherent. All they do is answer each question, string their answers together, and voilà! You have a five-star review that helps move your law firm up the search rankings!

If you take anything away from this chapter, I want it to be that one email script. Tailor it to your area of law practice and clientele, and send away. I firmly believe that if you spend money on internet marketing, but ignore reviews, you're wasting your money. Reviews are *that* important.

So, syndicate your high-value content, save your law clients from certain disaster, and hire a quality marketing company to do everything else, such as SEO (more on this in the next chapter). And while you're at it, don't forget to take a peek at your online reviews once in a while. You may just find a way to quadruple your client intake by the end of the week.

Chapter 9
You Get Paid To Think, Marketers Get Paid To Do

How Not To Hire a Marketing Company: The Story of Results-First-Ryan

I know what you're thinking. Why talk about HIRING a marketing company when you've spent the last eight chapters teaching me how to market my law firm myself?!

Easy. The point of marketing (and of this book) is to grow your law firm. Provide value and distribute that value, and that's exactly what you'll do. And when you do, you'll have so many clients, you won't have the time you once did—and let's face it, you're already strapped! You're a professional legal expert, not a professional marketer. Once you get into the content creation groove you'll see what works for you and what doesn't. And you'll want to keep what does and quit everything else. Then you may want to try new things. More social media advertisements, new bait, different landing pages, an updated website, and more.

As a lawyer, you get paid to think. Other people get paid to do. Like a competent marketing company, for instance. One that you can hand the lead generation reigns over to, and trust they'll do a better job than you could. But marketing companies make an appearance in this book's subtitle because most of them screw their clients over. Look at our buddy, Ryan:

Ryan M <resultfirstryan@gmail.com>
Mon, Jan 18, 2016, 2:41 AM

From: Ryan M <resultfirstryan@gmail.com>
Telephone: 619-███████

Message Body:
Thomas, I am contacting you to see if you would be interested in 100% FREE TRIAL where I work to get your website on the 1st page of Google, Yahoo and Bing. There are no up-front fees and I only get paid if I can get your website to page 1. I have over 6 years of experience working with Lawyers. If you would be interested in more information just shoot me an email back at resultfirstryan@████████ or call me at 619-███ ███████. Thanks, Ryan

--
This e-mail was sent from a contact form on ████████

One of my clients recently received the above email. In fact, every single one of my clients has heard from Ryan over the years. Maybe you have, too. On a surface level, he makes an unbeatable offer—"I don't charge any up-front fees, and you only pay if I can get you the page one results you want." Ryan does the work, and if it doesn't work out, you don't pay.

Yes, all that smart content on your blog *will* consistently increase your website traffic over time. But you want the God's honest truth? *No* legitimate marketing company can guarantee a specific rank for any given set of keywords. (The only exception to that rule is your name or your law firm's name, but those don't really count.)

Results-First-Ryan doesn't tell you that he uses the SEO equivalent of spam. Just as email services eventually catch (and stop) spammers, Google will look for you. They will find you. And they will kill your ranking. You may sneak past RankBrain for a couple of days—just long enough for your check to clear Ryan's bank account. Then when your site gets hit with penalties, you won't get any replies from Results-First-Ryan. He probably didn't even *see* your eleven emails and five voicemails because he's too busy enjoying a bottomless margarita in Cancún.

In spite of hacks like Ryan who ruin lawyers' websites, it can still make sense to delegate marketing tasks to a third party—should you choose to do SEO. I don't talk a lot about how to do SEO in this book because it's always changing. From the time I started writing this book to publishing it, Google made more than *nine* major search engine algorithm updates. That's why you want a competent internet marketing company that specializes in SEO to do it for you. They'll be up-to-date and know exactly how to get you noticed in organic searches.

If you're really interested in tackling SEO on your own, you can get a free guide that shows the steps to getting your law firm ranked on Google at www.getlawfirmclients.com/seo.

As you know, I get attorneys all across North America trying to hire me. The one percent of ethical marketers out there get ninety-nine percent of the business. Personally, I'm not taking on new clients, but I *can* help you navigate the marketing services waters. With so many new SEO tools, tips, and tactics available, it's hard not to crash into an "expert" who's all hype and no substance.

Just as you're a partner to your clients, the real marketers who can genuinely boost your bottom line see themselves as *your* long-term partner. Notice how quick Results-First-Ryan wants to get you results? It's attractive, isn't it? Like a hot date. But it doesn't go anywhere. Like marriage, true partnership requires long-term commitment. That's why you want to keep your standards high. The last thing you want is your law firm dragging some marketer through a messy divorce. To find and court the real deal, you're going to keep your standards high.

You already know the law firms at the top of the Google search results aren't necessarily the best lawyers. Don't get me wrong, that doesn't mean that you can't be a good lawyer and appear at the top of the Google search results. What it *does* mean is those law firms typically have a very high quality, highly skilled SEO company. Yet, I talk to law firms all the time that are on their fourth, fifth, even sixth marketing company. While there are a lot of companies out there just selling snake oil, there are also a lot of good companies worth hiring.

So, how can you tell them apart and avoid the hire-then-fire scenario I see so many lawyers play out? The best ways to determine if an internet marketing company can help you is to talk to their clients and to look at their numbers. SEO provides precise numbers and percentages. You don't have to rely on impressions or anecdotes to determine if a marketing company is the real deal. It's black and white. If a marketing company has success and the statistics to prove it, they'll be happy to share those numbers with you.

And they'll *tell* you the most important metrics to track without you having to ask. Why? Because they market their own marketing company. They practice what they preach. You can find out if an agency is legitimate or not without having to reach out to them, in many cases. If their website looks like it was thrown together in five minutes, it probably was. Quality SEO companies have social media profiles that match the look and feel of their (good) website. They post high value content regularly. They have dozens of client testimonials. Super-detailed positive feedback outweighs petty complaints. The website contact page features a questionnaire that helps their team understand your needs before they talk to you.

When you engage a marketing company, go into full vetting mode. Just because they passed the first test—a web presence inspection, for example—doesn't mean they won't bomb on a call with you. So get a company decision maker on the phone, and ask questions to determine if they're the right partner for your law firm. *Like what, Andy?* Good question. Here are several questions I always recommend you ask your potential marketing company. Most relate to SEO, which is a big part of the marketing they'd handle for you.

What Are the Payments Terms?

The contract arrangement should be clearly beneficial to both parties. Make certain that you fully understand and that you're comfortable with the way you'll pay for the services. Will there be a retainer? Are you paying a monthly fee or is there another arrangement? Are services bundled? Can payments be made online? You'll have to consider these questions and find the answers—and the marketing professionals—that are right for you.

Do You Offer Discounts?

This one is actually a trick question. Remember, no top-notch internet marketing company offers discounts. They don't have to. People looking for a bargain only find companies that promise the moon. If you ask this question and get push back, you know they take their own work seriously.

What Will You Do To Improve Our Firm's Google Rankings?

A marketing company is going to have some type of strategy to optimize your website for search engines. That program will almost always include a strategy of building backlinks from other websites to your website. (When someone posts a link on *their* website to *your* website, that's called a backlink.) That's because backlinks are still a very important part of Google's algorithm. It's very important to have high-quality backlinks going to your website.

But not all backlinks are created equal. One good strategy is called "outreach linking." The marketing company reaches out to other blogs and websites who also target your niche. They pitch them your site as a "trusted legal resource," and they link to you. If the company you're talking to mentions "outreach linking" to build your backlinks, that's another good sign they know what they're doing.

Now, I don't cover an "outreach linking how-to" in this book because, as you can imagine, it's a time-consuming, difficult, expensive strategy. You have better things to do. You have cases to handle and clients to help. Let a full-time marketer handle it. And they *should* handle it. Google *loves* authentic backlinks from real websites.

Sketchy marketing companies don't want to go through the trouble of building backlinks one at a time, so they automate the process. The result? Hundreds of low-quality backlinks that have no search engine value. If the strategy the marketing company suggests involves building automated links in a short period of time, that's a red flag. The marketer will likely do a lot of busy work, but it won't impact your Google rankings. Take a pass. You want quality over quantity.

Can You Give Me Information About Previous Clients And What You've Done For Them?

Hiring an internet marketing company is no different than hiring a contractor to work on your house. Any good contractor is happy to show you testimonials from satisfied customers. They'll also point you to online reviews and show samples of successful projects that they've completed in the past.

A quality marketing company is willing to do the same. If the company can't or won't give proof of work they've done for attorneys in the past, that's another red flag. They're either lying about their expertise or their experience—or both. You don't want them anywhere near your law firm.

You can also ask the company how long they've been with their oldest client. If the marketing company helps a firm grow, they will *absolutely* retain the marketing company year after year. Shady marketing companies are hit and run operations and don't have long-term clients. They often use short-term SEO tactics that (in the long run) do more harm than good. This means they won't be able to point to examples of long-term, highly satisfied clients.

Do You Follow the Rules? Do You Keep Up With Algorithm Updates?

This is a tricky one. Technically, if you're doing anything to manipulate your rankings, it could be considered against Google's guidelines. However, there's a fine line between white hat, black hat, and grey hat, which is a mixture of the two. ("White hat" refers to any tactic that follows a platform's terms of service, like Google. "Black hat" tactics break the rules and get you penalized. "Grey hat" means you get to do a little of both.)

In general, Google looks for high-quality, unique website content. Google also says that if you build high-quality websites with great content, you won't need SEO— you'll just rank high naturally. But like a lot of things, that's not exactly true. Even great websites often need some help getting there, and that's where search engine optimization comes in. Any good marketing company is going to have a very good understanding of the Google guidelines. They're going to know how far they can push the envelope and they're going to be in control of the campaign the entire time. They should be intimately familiar with the Google algorithm updates. That way their clients can take advantage of all the latest updates, while avoiding any of the negative consequences.

There have been many Google algorithm updates over the years, but the two most popular are Panda and Penguin. Panda prevents websites with poor quality content from finding their way to the top of the search results. Penguin catches websites that artificially raise their search rankings using spammy websites.

A high quality internet marketing company should understand how to avoid penalties. So, when you're interviewing a potential marketing company, ask them how they follow the guidelines and how they keep track of the updates. If they can't give you a satisfactory (and simple) answer, move on.

What Type Of Website Optimization Will You Do?

There are typically three answers the marketer can give to this question. Technical optimization, on-site optimization, and off-site optimization. Technical SEO is looking for technical problems on your site that prevent it from ranking on Google. Off-page SEO focuses on authoritative, relevant backlinks. On-page SEO focuses on your website content. If I've lost your focus with this one, don't worry. A good internet marketing company should be able to discuss (and handle) the details of all three of these strategies with your firm.

Do You Guarantee Us A Number One Ranking On Google?

This is another trick question that helps you separate fly-by-night marketers from the legit companies. *No one* can guarantee you the number one ranking on Google—because no marketing company or marketer knows the exact Google algorithm! *Not even Google!*

In SEO, things change quickly. No serious marketer can guarantee *anything*. So if you hear guarantees, it's time to end the interview. The only exception to this rule is for extremely easy keywords, such as your law firm name.

What's Your Procedure For Keeping Us In The Loop About Activity And Results?

You and the marketing company should meet on a regular basis to discuss all activity, as well as the results that you see on your end. My company meets monthly with every single one of our clients. We discuss what we've done, what we plan to do, and the results the client has seen.

You should always be kept in the loop and meet regularly with the marketing company. This way, you know exactly what they're doing, and they can track your results. If the company's not willing to meet with you on a regular basis, then they don't want you to know what they're doing. That's never a good sign.

What Happens If We Terminate Services?

Most internet marketing companies want a contract for their services. It makes sense, because a lot of work goes in upfront. Often, search engine optimization doesn't happen right away. Almost all internet marketing companies that are worth their salt will require at least a six-month or year-long contract. That said, at the end of the term, you might want to end your contract and find a new marketing company. It's important that you understand what will happen should things go south with the company.

Expect a termination policy. Find out what the procedure is for winding down your relationship, should you ever want to. Look for any early termination clauses in the contract. And make sure that you own the website, the content, and the images on the website. Otherwise, you could leave with nothing. Talk about being on the wrong end of a messy divorce.

How Do You Fix Penalized Websites?

Google constantly updates their algorithm, which sometimes results in a penalized website. Even if you didn't do anything wrong! An established marketing company will likely have experience recovering penalized websites. It's critical that they understand how to do it, because even if you've done nothing wrong, your website could still get hit by a penalty. Mistakes happen. Sometimes you just have bad luck and get hit by an algorithm update. Find out what procedures the company takes to resuscitate penalized sites and find out what they do to prevent future penalties.

What Metrics Do You Use To Determine Success?

You're hiring an internet marketing company to improve your bottom line. Whether or not that happens (or to what extent it happens) will determine if the company is successful for you. Understand which metrics this company uses to determine their own success. They may consider an increase in traffic or ranking a success, but you're looking to get more law clients. Period. An increase in traffic and rankings are great, but those two metrics alone do not put money in the bank. A good marketing company will look at ROI and conversions as their metric for success. For example, my company, Social Firestarter, measures success by ROI, phone calls, and new cases.

Why Should I Hire Your Marketing Company Over Another Marketing Company?

Listen for deal-breaking answers. "We're cheaper than the competition," "We guarantee number rankings," "We can get you thousands of backlinks," or "We get results faster than anyone else." Ain't a flag high enough or red enough. A good marketing company points out past accomplishments and a list of satisfied clients instead.

What Platform Will My Website Be Built On?

I prefer websites built in WordPress, as it's the most user-friendly content management system out there. While WordPress isn't the end-all-be-all, you should avoid marketing companies that expect you to use *their* website platform. Listen for that trigger word— *proprietary*. Hear a marketer use that word when referencing the website they'll be building for you, and you'll want to move right along.

Why, you ask? Isn't "proprietary" typically a selling point? If a marketing company builds your website using their proprietary system, *they* own your website. Period. You'll have to start over with a brand new website if you ever part ways with that marketer. They may give you a consolation prize—the website files that you'll have to send to a programmer to rebuild your website. Better to avoid this headache if you can.

What Happens If We Don't See Results?

Here's the truth no marketer wants to admit: you may hire the best marketing company in the world, they may do a phenomenal job, and you still may not get results. Unfortunately, that's how search engine optimization is sometimes. Google can't be controlled. It's ridiculously frustrating.

Should this happen, you need to know how the company plans to handle it. Ask them what they've done in the past when their best efforts haven't gone as planned. Ask them if they're willing to supplement with PPC or social media ads if needed. They should be able to support you in implementing every lead generation strategy covered in this book while still building your SEO. After all, they should want you to succeed as much as you do. Happy clients are long-term clients—the bread and butter of every reputable marketing company.

Ultimately, modern marketing is a long-term investment in the future profitability of your firm. There are no quick fixes or instant results. It can take weeks for any marketing strategy to show that it works…or doesn't. That's one of the main reasons why so many sub-par marketing companies exist. They suck their clients dry. By the time you realize they've ripped you off, they're on to the next victim, just like Results-First-Ryan. These questions will prevent that from happening to you. You can decide for yourself if a marketing company can boost your firm's revenue to the next level. Or if they're just looking to fund their next Caribbean booze cruise.

Chapter 10
Back to the Future (Of Law Firm Marketing)

YOUR Future

Forty years ago, lawyers advertised in newspapers and magazines. Thirty years ago, attorneys took to the radio and TV airwaves. Twenty years ago, law firms bought promotions in the Yellow Pages. Ten years ago (and up to the present day), lawyers have tried to beat Google at their own SEO game and get traction on the social media platform du jour. Through the ages, only one thing remains constant —**value wins**.

When you read this book a decade from now, Facebook may be a has-been. But everything you now know about creating value, distributing that value, and following up with people who consume your value? *It'll work like a CHARM.*

Today, tomorrow, and for years to come, the attorneys who will dominate online lead generation will be those who go the extra mile. They're different from other lawyers. They swim in a virtually competition-free ocean. In the future, it won't be a question of which strategy works, it'll be which channel, medium, or platform works. That's why I've kept these chapters as strategic processes versus step by step tactics. Anybody can publish *The Annual Guide to Social Media Advertising*, and dozens of marketing companies do. Before the ink is dry, the book's outdated. But lead with value, and your marketing is as timeless as the legal profession itself.

As technology changes, so will what sets you apart from competitors. The most successful law firms in the future will be the most creative, innovative, and outside-the-box. To help you future-proof your law firm, I want to close out this book with three revolutionary strategies you won't find anyone else doing right now.

Self-Liquidate Your Offer

Earlier in this book, you learned how to launch your first high-converting social media advertising campaign. What if you wanted to keep advertising but not pay *one cent*? It's possible with a Self-Liquidating Offer, such as a "Free Plus Shipping & Handling" deal. Here's what I mean.

I created a Facebook advertising training on a USB drive and gave it to lawyers for free via a (you guessed it) Facebook ad. I charged $9.97 for shipping the USB, and thousands of lawyers all across North America begged me to send them one. The shipping and handling cost actually covered the cost of the USBs ($3 each) *and* my advertising budget. To keep my conversion rates high, I offered a money-back guarantee: "The USB arrives undamaged *and* you love the training...or your money back." I didn't have a single refund request.

When you follow this exact same strategy, include an appointment request form on the shipping page. That way, once someone requests your USB with free education about the laws affecting them (AKA, what your niche cares about), you'll get free leads right away. It can be a ten-part video series like the daily content you're already creating. For example, if you're an estate planning attorney, talk about the process for drawing up an estate and how not to screw up your financial legacy.

Why not put the free material online? People assign more value to a physical object than digital content. Plus, if they spend $9.97, you now have a buyer. And someone who buys once is way more likely to buy again.

If a USB drive isn't your thing, choose a physical product like a credit card shaped bottle opener, if you're a DUI attorney. Your name and contact information appears on the product. If the person gets pulled over and arrested, legal help is right there inside their wallet. Personal injury lawyer? Go with a cell phone holder that sticks onto a windshield or dashboard. Get your name and contact info printed smack dab on the holder so when the worst case scenario happens, you are right in front of them.

Whether you go with a USB drive, a credit card shaped bottle opener, a cell phone holder, or something else, I've got you covered on the offer itself. You don't have to figure out how to put together your Self-Liquidating Offer landing page. I've taken care of the hard part.

Get your free template for my
Self-Liquidating Offer right here:
www.getlawfirmclients.com/resources

Light Up Your Lead Generation

A long time ago, I was in a rock band. To promote my band, I put our logo on lighters with bottle openers. Before and after every gig, my buddies passed them around to patrons at the bars and nightclubs where we performed. Years later, I suggested the idea to a criminal defense attorney client on a budget.

"Get a box of lighters for a buck a piece. Have a promotional items company put your logo on them, go to every local bar, and give a box of one or two hundred to the bartender to pass out to patrons. Many people who drink also smoke...one substance or another."

He followed my advice, spent $600, and scored a few DUI clients right away. Steal this idea for your law firm. If you purchase promotional products, make sure they are something that your ideal client actually wants (again, always providing value). For example, lighters and bottle openers are things people actually hang on to. Always make sure your name, the type of law you practice, and your phone number appear on the item. Distribute them at locations where you know your niche hangs out. For DUI niche attorneys, lighters with a built-in bottle opener work best because almost every lighter will reach two to three people, minimum (just ask a smoker how hard it is to keep a lighter). In the months ahead, your brand will be top of mind—and right in front of your next client when they need your legal services. Well worth the minimal cost.

Test drive new, innovative marketing ideas like these, and you set up your firm for insane success. A lot will change in the coming years, and many firms will go out of business. That's why you owe it to yourself—and to the clients you'll serve (and *save*) in the years ahead—to look into my marketing crystal ball. As the Greek philosopher Heraclitus told us:

Change is the only constant in life.[1]

How drastic is that change? *Pretty damn drastic*, if you ask me, especially for anyone marketing a law firm in the years ahead.

THE Future

On May 25, 2018, the European Union General Data Protection Regulation (GDPR) took effect. If your business is located in Europe (or if any of your customers are), the rules changed overnight. This new strict law upended how companies handle prospect, lead, and customer data.[2] We're talking names, contact info, transaction details, web activity, social profiles, IP addresses, and more here.

From that fateful day onward, EU customers hold new rights, such as the right to information access, the right to be forgotten, and the right to object. Companies now have to tell every individual how they've used their personal data when asked. And they have to do so immediately, completely, and totally free of charge. If a client no longer wants to be a client, the company is legally obligated to expunge their information permanently—and provide proof they did. And if anybody wants you to stop marketing to them forever, you have no choice but to oblige.

Talk about an operations migraine unlike anything we've ever seen. Don't play along, and your law firm faces fines of 4% of annual revenue or $23 *million*, whichever is greater. If you handled cases in Europe when GDPR went into effect, the high ethical standard attorneys already had to abide by got even higher. I foresee GDPR-like regulations coming to North America, the US specifically, within the next couple of decades. Attorney Brian Faughnan of Lewis Thomason in Memphis, Tennessee, paints a picture of what American lawyers have to "look forward" to:

> [Under GDPR] consent can no longer be a global consent but must specify the types of data and uses to which the subject is consenting. Lawyers are going to have to address this in their engagement letters...GDPR doesn't permit waiving consent.[3]

In other words, it's no longer okay to tell a client, "I'm keeping a copy of the files," if they ask you not to. Another ramification of Europe's new rules? GDPR effectively brought email campaigns to a complete halt—at least briefly. If even one email address you had on your list was EU-based, you had to send *another* opt-in email request to your entire email list. Remember when people hit your landing page, asked for your bait, and joined your email list? Well, in the world of GDPR, that's not good enough. So, it's imperative that you get as many email addresses as you can *now* and start providing tons of value. That way, when GDPR comes to America, potential clients will *already* be used to getting your value. They won't be able to imagine *not* keeping you around in their inbox! Say, "Opt in to continue receiving our emails," and your list goes, "Well, duh, of course, yes!"

GDPR isn't the only pending disruption I see on the horizon. The algorithms behind SEO get smarter and smarter every *second*. In five years, we'll have no hope of beating Google at their own game. There is (that is, there *will be*) good news. Lawyers with user-generated content (e.g., clients reviews) will rank ever higher in search results, beating those who try to game Google.

And if that's not crazy enough, yet *another* change will take you by storm—your local competition. Because sooner or later, they'll get their hands on this book, too. Then you won't be the only attorney in town with a Second Amendment advocate criminal defense law Facebook group. Or the traumatic brain injury patients community. Or that family and friends of addicts support group.

Since competition to provide the most free high-value content *is* coming, all you can do is do it first. Aim for good enough, *not* perfect. In marketing, we call that the first mover principle. Move quick and corner a new opportunity before anyone else, and you win all the chips. It doesn't matter if you're a one-person law firm like Renee. And it doesn't matter if you don't have a Hollywood recording studio to shoot videos. You win big because you got there first. Welcome to your own blue ocean, my friend.

So, what *does* matter? Getting started. Providing value *today*. And getting used to doing it. I know, I know—just starting is the hardest part, but you don't need to burn yourself out like you did with that new workout routine. (Haven't we all been there?) Make a goal of recording a short video every day this week. If you're feeling nervous, flip back to Chapter 6 to remind yourself that you don't have to (or even *want* to!) be perfect. Reach out to five clients and get reviews. Grab my template for asking clients for reviews from Chapter 8. Start your group and invite ten past clients. Revisit Chapter 5 if you need a refresher.

The VERY Next Step

To get the most out of this book, it's essential you do the following three things:

Join the free Lawyer Marketing Facebook Group at www.getlawfirmclients.com/group.

Watch the supplemental training webinar to immediately put this book into practice. Go to www.getlawfirmclients.com/training.

Book a free fifteen-minute strategy session with me at www.getlawfirmclients.com/meet

And for a little extra motivation, just imagine—*whatever you do today will improve your practice two weeks from now*. Of course, you don't have to imagine. Because soon you'll see for yourself that it's true. It'll be true twenty years from now, too. And to paraphrase Heraclitus, the only *two* constants in life are change...and *value*.

Notes

Chapter 1

1. Rampton, John. "20 Life Changing Quotes by Tony Robbins." Inc.com. July 25, 2016. Accessed November 15, 2018. https://www.inc.com/john-rampton/20-life-changing-quotes-by-tony-robbins.html.

2. Stewart, Emily. "Donald Trump Rode $5 Billion in Free Media to the White House." The Street. November 20, 2016. Accessed November 15, 2018. https://www.thestreet.com/story/13896916/1/donald-trump-rode-5-billion-in-free-media-to-the-white-house.html.

3. Pinola, Melanie. ""A Year from Now You May Wish You Had Started Today"." Lifehacker. June 24, 2013. Accessed November 15, 2018. https://lifehacker.com/5985612/a-year-from-now-you-may-wish-you-had-started-today

4. "Woody Allen's Success Secret." Persistence Unlimited RSS. Accessed November 15, 2018. http://persistenceunlimited.com/2006/03/woody-allens-success-secret/.

Chapter 2

1. "Top Earning Websites | Most Profitable Websites." How To Make Money Online. April 19, 2018. Accessed November 15, 2018. https://www.incomediary.com/top-earning-websites.

2. "Understanding Legal Consumers." Digital image. FindLaw. February 2018. Accessed November 27, 2018. https://www.lawyermarketing.com/wp-

content/uploads/2018/02/FindLaw_2017LegalConsumer_Infogr
aphic.jpg.

3. Mozes, Alan. "1 in 5 College Students Admitted to Drunk
    Driving, Study Found." Consumer HealthDay. June 02, 2010.
    Accessed November 15, 2018.
    https://consumer.healthday.com/kids-health-information-
    23/kids-and-alcohol-health-news-11/1-in-5-college-students-
    admitted-to-drunk-driving-study-found-639483.html.

4. The Canadian Press. "Motorcyclists 10 times More Likely to
    Suffer Serious Injuries in Collisions than Car Drivers."
    Thestar.com. November 20, 2017. Accessed November 15,
    2018.
    https://www.thestar.com/news/canada/2017/11/20/motorcycl
    ists-10-times-more-likely-to-suffer-serious-injuries-in-collisions-
    than-car-drivers.html.

5. Robbins, Tony. "Most People Overestimate What They Can Do
    in a Year and They Underestimate What They Can Do in Two or
    Three Decades. #iamnotyourguru." Twitter. October 25, 2016.
    Accessed November 15, 2018.
    https://twitter.com/tonyrobbins/status/790937782784970752?
    lang=en.

Chapter 3

1. Womack, Justin. "Your Moral Obligation To Identify Your Ideal
    Client." Marketing And Growth Hacking. April 17, 2018.
    Accessed November 15, 2018.
    https://blog.markgrowth.com/lets-face-it-not-all-customers-
    are-created-equal-why-everyone-is-not-your-customer-
    cb1335e75e9d.

2. "Mobile Share of Website Visits Worldwide 2018 | Statistic." Statista. Accessed November 15, 2018. https://www.statista.com/statistics/241462/global-mobile-phone-website-traffic-share/.

3. "Email Continues to Deliver Strong ROI and Value for Marketers." EMarketer. September 12, 2016. Accessed November 15, 2018. https://www.emarketer.com/Article/Email-Continues-Deliver-Strong-ROI-Value-Marketers/1014461.

4. Abraham, Jay. *The Sticking Point Solution: 9 Ways to Move Your Business from Stagnation to Stunning Growth in Tough Economic Times*. Philadelphia, PA: Vanguard Press, 2010.

Chapter 4

1. Warren, Blair. *The One Sentence Persuasion Course - 27 Words to Make the World Do Your Bidding*. 1st ed. Blair Warren, 2013. December 18, 2013. Accessed November 15, 2018. https://www.amazon.com/One-Sentence-Persuasion-Course-Bidding-ebook/dp/B00AAF5GJK.

Chapter 5

1. Canal, Emily. "We Fact-Checked Seven Seasons Of Shark Tank Deals. Here Are The Results." Forbes. November 02, 2016. Accessed November 15, 2018. https://www.forbes.com/sites/emilycanal/2016/10/21/about-72-of-deals-that-happen-on-shark-tank-dont-turn-out-as-seen-on-tv/#71ed78c4ed14.

2. Abraham, Jay. "People Are Silently Begging to Be Led. They're Crying out to Know More about Your Product/service. Educate Them - See Your Profits Soar!" Twitter. July 27, 2012. Accessed

November 15, 2018.
https://twitter.com/realjayabraham/status/2289311808195133
45.

3. "Bringing People Closer Together." Facebook Newsroom.
    Accessed November 15, 2018.
    https://newsroom.fb.com/news/2018/01/news-feed-fyi-
    bringing-people-closer-together/.

4. Kolowich, Lindsay. "The Best Time to Post on Instagram,
    Facebook, Twitter, LinkedIn, Pinterest, and Google
    [Infographic]." HubSpot Blog. Accessed November 15, 2018.
    https://blog.hubspot.com/marketing/best-times-post-pin-
    tweet-social-media-infographic.

Chapter 6

1. "Email Marketing Benchmarks By Industry: CTR, Bounce Rate,
    Open Rate." Linchpin SEO. November 02, 2018. Accessed
    November 15, 2018. https://linchpinseo.com/email-marketing-
    benchmarks-industry/.

Chapter 7

1. Weisul, Kimberly. "Mark Cuban's Top 3 Rules for Business
    Success...and 1 Secret." Inc.com. May 20, 2015. Accessed
    November 15, 2018. https://www.inc.com/kimberly-
    weisul/mark-cuban-three-rules-business-success-one-
    secret.html.

Chapter 8

1. Bahareth, Mohammad. Kings of the Internet: What You Don't Know about Them ? IUniverse, Incorporated, 2012.

2. "88% Of Consumers Trust Online Reviews As Much As Personal Recommendations." Search Engine Land. December 26, 2014. Accessed November 15, 2018. https://searchengineland.com/88-consumers-trust-online-reviews-much-personal-recommendations-195803.

3. Wallace, Chantelle. "How Clients Use Online Legal Reviews." Software Advice. Accessed November 15, 2018. https://www.softwareadvice.com/legal/industryview/how-clients-use-legal-reviews-2014/.

4. "Impact of Reviews and Ratings on Search Click-Through Rates." BrightLocal. Accessed November 15, 2018. https://www.brightlocal.com/learn/review-search-click-through-study/.

5. Sivers, Derek. "Keep Your Goals to Yourself." TED. Accessed November 15, 2018. https://www.ted.com/talks/derek_sivers_keep_your_goals_to_yourself?language=en.

6. Farivar, Cyrus. "Yelp Settles Suit with Bankruptcy Lawyer over Allegations of Fake Reviews." Ars Technica. October 02, 2015. Accessed November 15, 2018. https://arstechnica.com/tech-policy/2015/10/yelp-settles-lawsuit-with-bankruptcy-over-allegations-of-fake-reviews/.

7. Associated Press. "Yelp Tactics Are 'at Most, Hard Bargaining' and Not Illegal, Judge Says." The Mercury News. August 12, 2016. Accessed November 15, 2018.

https://www.mercurynews.com/2014/09/04/yelp-tactics-are-at-most-hard-bargaining-and-not-illegal-judge-says/.

8. Labay, Ben. "Do Review Stars on Google Help Click-Through Rate? [Original Study]." CXL. October 26, 2017. Accessed November 15, 2018. https://conversionxl.com/research-study/review-stars-google-help-click-rate-study/.

Chapter 10

1. Mark, Joshua J. "Heraclitus of Ephesus." Ancient History Encyclopedia. July 14, 2010. Accessed November 15, 2018. https://www.ancient.eu/Heraclitus_of_Ephesos/.

2. "GDPR: What Is It and How Does It Impact My Business?" CRM Blog: Articles, Tips and Strategies by SuperOffice. November 14, 2018. Accessed November 15, 2018. https://www.superoffice.com/blog/gdpr/.

3. Gunnarsson, Helen. "U. S. Law Firms Must Prepare For GDPR, Panel Warns." Big Law Business. February 21, 2018. Accessed September 5, 2018. https://biglawbusiness.com/u-s-law-firms-must-prepare-for-gdpr-panel-warns/.

Get a free MP3 player with audio from over one hundred of
my YouTube marketing videos. Headphones Included!

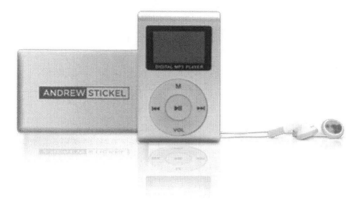

All you have to do is record a video testimonial telling me how this book helps you.
Then go to mp3.andrewstickel.com, upload your video, and fill out the form.

A lot of times people want to leave a review but aren't quite sure what to say.
Below are some questions that should give you some ideas and will make your
review more helpful to other lawyers reading the book.

1. What was the problem you had before you read this book?

2. Why did you choose this book?

3. What makes this book so effective?

4. As a result of implementing the strategies in this book, what was your
    outcome?

5. How has your life changed since achieving this outcome?

The more detail you can provide the better, but if you're short on time or
inspiration I'd still love a shorter review.